André Breton: Selections. Edited and with an Introduction by Mark Polizzotti

María Sabina: Selections. Edited by Jerome Rothenberg. With Translations and Commentaries by Álvaro Estrada and Others

Paul Celan: Selections. Edited and with an Introduction by Pierre Joris

José Lezama Lima: Selections. Edited and with an Introduction by Ernesto Livon-Grosman

Miyazawa Kenji: Selections. Edited and with an Introduction by Hiroaki Sato

*The publisher gratefully acknowledges the generous contribution
to this book provided by the Literature in Translation Endowment Fund
of the University of California Press Foundation, which is
supported by a major gift from Joan Palevsky.*

MIYAZAWA KENJI

SELECTIONS

MIYAZAWA KENJI

EDITED AND WITH AN INTRODUCTION BY

HIROAKI SATO

UNIVERSITY OF CALIFORNIA PRESS

Berkeley   Los Angeles   London

University of California Press, one of the most distinguished university presses
in the United States, enriches lives around the world by advancing scholarship in the
humanities, social sciences, and natural sciences. Its activities are supported by the
UC Press Foundation and by philanthropic contributions from individuals
and institutions. For more information, visit www.ucpress.edu.

University of California Press
Berkeley and Los Angeles, California

University of California Press, Ltd.
London, England

Credits and acknowledgments for the poems and other texts included are on page 247.

Library of Congress Cataloging-in-Publication Data

Miyazawa, Kenji, 1896–1933.
[Selections. English. 2007]
Miyazawa Kenji : selections / edited and with an introduction by Hiroaki Sato.
p.   cm. — (Poets for the millennium ; 5)
Includes bibliographical references.
ISBN 978-0-520-24470-2 (cloth : alk. paper)
ISBN 978-0-520-24779-6 (pbk. : alk. paper)
1. Miyazawa, Kenji, 1896–1933 — Translations into English.
2. Miyazawa, Kenji, 1896–1933 — Criticism and interpretation.
I. Sato, Hiroaki, 1942–.   II. Title.
PL833.I95A6   2007

895.6'344 — dc22   2006025555

Manufactured in the United States of America
16   15   14   13   12   11   10   09   08   07
10   9   8   7   6   5   4   3   2   1

This book is printed on Natures Book, which contains 50% post-consumer waste and meets
the minimum requirements of ANSI/NISO Z39.48–1992 (R 1997) (Permanence of Paper).

CONTENTS

POEMS

ILLUSTRATIONS

GEOFFREY O'BRIEN

The Japanese poet Miyazawa Kenji, who died in 1933 at the age of thirty-seven, became a culture hero on the strength of a single brief poem written toward the end of his obscure and voluntarily impoverished life. "November 3rd" — an unpublished notebook entry probably intended more as a prayer than a poem — sketches a portrait of an idealized ascetic:

> neither yielding to rain
> nor yielding to wind
> . . . .
> without greed
> never getting angry
> always smiling quiet-
> > ly
> eating one and a half pints of brown rice
> and bean paste and a bit of
> > vegetables a day
> in everything
> not taking oneself
> > into account

and concludes:

                    someone
                              like that
        is what I want
                    to be

Revered as a religious utterance, exploited in the 1940s as a wartime morale booster promoting self-sacrifice, and memorized by every subsequent generation of schoolchildren, "November 3rd" remains universally familiar in a way that no poem has in the West since Rudyard Kipling's "If" or Joyce Kilmer's "Trees." The world it evokes, a world of thatched huts and drought-stricken fields, sickly children and rice farmers with bent backs, might appear anachronistic when set against the Japan of computer graphics and advanced robot technology — unless you were to take a bus into the mountains and see landscapes and faces lifted intact from a Miyazawa poem.

In his own way Miyazawa came quite close to realizing the saintly ideal set forth in "November 3rd." The son of a pawnbroker in northern Japan's Iwate Prefecture (a backward region afflicted with chronic crop failures), he converted in adolescence to the Nichiren sect of Buddhism. Taking as his guide the Lotus Sutra, which teaches the availability of Buddhahood to all sentient beings, he dedicated himself to the welfare of the local farmers, becoming a sort of one-man cultural and agricultural missionary, teaching crop rotation and soil improvement and exploring methods of flood and drought prevention. In the meantime, he strictly observed vegetarianism, often subsisting on a poorer diet even than the local people were used to, and as a result he ruined his health.

Such a career clearly lends itself to hagiography, and it is somewhat ironic that Miyazawa has been claimed in turn by militarists, Buddhists, modernist aesthetes, and most recently (so Gary Snyder tells us) the Japanese Greens. All these claims occurred after the poet was safely dead: for Miyazawa was not the sort of person ever to become a leader or a spokesman. He was a strange mix of humility and irascibility, whimsy and anguish, and the self-imposed deprivations of his life contrast mysteriously with the exuberant profusion of his writing. His poems — he wrote several thousand, in both traditional and modern forms — range from epigrams to an eight-hundred-line free-verse notation of a journey on foot, from comic monologues to metaphysical reveries, from scientifically precise landscapes to fervent devotional outpourings, while his children's stories express sometimes surprisingly violent and tragic themes through a cast of animals, stars, and gods.

One of the most distinct poetic voices of this century, Miyazawa was one of the most private as well. A single self-published collection in 1924 was his only gesture toward making his poetry public, his life was lived apart from literary circles, and — notwithstanding the vigorous modernity of his style — he thought of his writing more in religious than aesthetic terms. He wrote at a time when Japanese poetry, after confining itself for a millennium or so to effusions of no more than thirty-three syllables, was branching out with gusto into the wide-open spaces of vers libre. But much of this work had a borrowed tone, heavy with Parnassian and Symbolist echoes and imbued with a certain lugubrious self-pity. Miyazawa — for whom self-pity was never a mild emotion but something closer to self-torture — nevertheless cultivated a bright, sharply defined, often comic diction, hurling incongruous elements together and letting them find their own unexpected unity.

Miyazawa used the title *Spring & Asura* for three separate collections of his poetry in modern forms. An asura is a demon, inhabiting one of the six Buddhist realms of existence, and the opposition of restless demon and vegetative landscape makes a fitting ideograph for Miyazawa's poetry, where consciousness erupts into its surroundings and mind does not merely contemplate the world but actively constructs it. Yet mind is also a construct:

> The phenomenon called "I"
> is a blue illumination
> of the hypothesized, organic alternating current lamp
> (a compound of all transparent ghosts)
> a blue illumination
> of the karmic alternating current lamp
> which flickers busily, busily
> with landscapes, with everyone
> yet remains lit with such assuredness
> (the light persists, the lamp lost)

Self, the organizing principle of consciousness, is fragmentary. The "I" of Miyazawa's diaristic voice charts its own disintegration into its compound elements: lava slopes, mineral deposits, parched reeds, foreign scientific terms, Sanskrit mantras, imaginary vistas of China or Italy or Russia, apparitions of Buddhist saints and demons, abstract patterns of line and color. (The expertise with which Miyazawa breaks down the world in his poems ties in curiously with his employment, in the last years of his life, as an engineer for a local rock-crushing company.) The wonder is that this disintegration of self leads not into a void but into an ecstatic fullness:

> Out of the gray steel of imagination
> akebi vines entwine the clouds,
> wildrose bush, humus marsh

begins the title poem "Spring & Asura," one of Miyazawa's most energetic flights:

> At the bottom of the light in April's atmospheric strata,
> spitting, gnashing, pacing back and forth,

I am Asura incarnate
  (the landscape sways in my tears)
Shattered clouds to the limit of visibility
  in heaven's sea of splendor
    sacred crystalline winds sweep
      spring's row of *Zypressen*
        absorbs ether, black,
          at its dark feet
            the snow ridge of Tien Shan glitters
              (waves of heat haze and white polarization)
              yet the True Words are lost
            the clouds, torn, fly through the sky.

He is devotional but never didactic. Despite the orthodoxy of his religious beliefs, one never gets the feeling that Miyazawa is limiting himself to what he ought to say. On the contrary, there is a nakedness and spontaneity leading to constant surprise. In the poems concerning the death of his sister Toshiko in November 1922 — including three written on the day itself — the grief is palpable and unpredictable in its manifestations. The death scene continues to well up in poems written the following year, along with visions of Toshiko assuming other forms:

Two large white birds fly
calling to each other sharply, sorrowfully
in the moist morning sunlight.
They are my sister,
my dead sister.

Elsewhere, as the wheels of a train squeak noisily and a moth crawls under a ceiling lamp, he writes:

My feelings are warped with sorrow
and I can't help thinking of her, hidden somewhere.

In the wake of her death, Miyazawa's poetry seems to toughen, mournful subjectivity hardening into mineral edge — "The sea is rusted by the morning's carbon acid" — and the poet taking a critical tone toward his own spiritual aspirations:

> Why do you try to grasp firmly in the human
> what you can get only in religion?
> . . . .
> Come now, wipe your tears, collect yourself.
> You must not love in so religious a mode.

Feeling, however intense, is not privileged over other levels of experience; it is a vehicle, not an end in itself. Many of Miyazawa's poems begin at a level of keyed-up emotion where someone else's would end and extend a mood of turmoil in almost leisurely fashion, as if the poet were sufficiently at home in his own anxieties to feel out the space around them and take notes on the view. His images suggest not so much the contents of his self as what remains after self has been exhausted. The world articulates itself in hard, jabbing lines: "The flock of crows is zinc scrap in dilute sulfuric acid." "Pale-blue sap oozes from the severed root." "The gray light avalanched in the distance." In the later poems the world enters more and more, bringing with it a varied population of animals (pigs, snakes, horses, insects) and humans whose doings are chronicled with almost novelistic density. A disheveled landlord, having loaned back the rice he's received as rent, goes off hunting to feed himself:

> But when he manages to haul back a bear,
> they say, "He killed the mountain god
> so this year's crop is poor."

A young doctor begins to integrate himself into village life, and Miyazawa suddenly sees him as he will be in a few years:

By the time this doctor finally comes to feel
just as the villagers do
. . . .
he'll have fallen behind in new techniques
and at the lecture of the county doctors' society
he'll curl up small, a perpetual listener.

The hallucinatory center of his poetry is framed by a broad, even humorous, picture of the surrounding community. He is not apart from the world but consciously alone in the midst of it, with all his senses operating.

The humor is chiefly evident in the monologues spoken by a series of bureaucratic or academic personae: "The Landscape Inspector," "Mr. Pamirs the Scholar Takes a Walk," "The Prefectural Engineer's Statement Regarding Clouds." Even in translation — or at least in translation as deft as Hiroaki Sato's — it is possible to gauge the juxtaposition of formulaic, ritually self-deprecating official language and the rugged, unresponsive landscape in whose midst it is spoken. Not surprisingly, the comedy has a bitter aftertaste, most memorably in "An Opinion Concerning a Proposed National Park Site," where the poet suggests turning his volcanic surroundings into a theme park embodying the Buddhist underworld:

And yes, here in particular, set up a Hell.
Make it charming the Oriental fashion.
A spear-shaped red fence.
Touch it up with dead trees starkly
. . . .
from Yama's Courthouse to the Womb-Trip —
. . . .
As a finale, blast off real shots electrically
from two field cannons
hidden this side of the mountain.

The moment they think, *Bingo!*
they're right there in the Three-Way River, you see.

In fact where he is—"this prefecture where there's nothing to eat"—is a lot tougher than Hell: "Over there on the frozen riverbed/ a naked baby was found abandoned." The flights of fantastic invention always return to their source. What separates Miyazawa's poetry most strikingly from that of most of his modernist contemporaries in Europe and America is its immersion in actual hunger and actual labor. The imminence of drought or flood and the murderous difficulty of procuring sustenance can be felt in every line.

In the later poems, physical work is the abiding and obsessive theme, not work on behalf of some idealized nation-state or political program but for bare survival. The anguish is no longer metaphysical but practical: "I'm filled with anxieties about the manure/I threw from the horse cart and left on the slope yesterday" (from "Work," in *Spring & Asura*). He monitors weather and growth as if vigilantly surveying the movements of a potential enemy:

> I calculate again and again
> the number of days before the delayed rice takes root,
> the number of days before bifurcation, and the time when the ears will
>   come out.

The real threat of starvation makes for the force of "The Breeze Comes Filling the Valley," a cry of triumph that, in the face of an anticipated crop failure and despite a violent flood of rain,

> because of the slight differences in seedling preparation
> and in the use of superphosphate,
> all the stalks are up today.

The triumph is only temporary, tentative — there will always be another season to worry about — but for the moment Miyazawa allows himself a moment of pure elation:

> I went home late at night.
> But in the end I did not sleep.
> And, look,
> this morning the east, the golden rose, opens,
> the clouds, the beacons, rise one after another,
> the high-voltage wires roar,
> the stagnant fog runs in the distance.
> The rice stalks have risen at last.
> They are living things,
> precision machines.
> All stand erect.
> At their tips, which waited patiently in the rain,
> tiny white flowers glisten
> and above the quiet amber puddles reflecting the sun
> red dragonflies glide.

Yet this plenitude — literal, not metaphoric — is after all only another moment of reality, no more privileged than the others that Miyazawa recorded. On the day of his death six years later, this tanka was the last poem he wrote:

> Because of an illness, crumbling
>   this life —
> if I could give it for the dharma
>   how glad I would be.

Gary Snyder was the first to translate a body of Miyazawa Kenji's poems into English. In the 1960s, Snyder, then living in Kyoto and pursuing Buddhism, was offered a grant to translate Japanese literature. He sought Burton Watson's opinion, and Watson, a scholar of Chinese classics trained at the University of Kyoto, recommended Kenji.[1] Snyder had first heard about Kenji a decade earlier, while he was attending the Buddhist Study Center in Berkeley, when Jane Imamura, the wife of the center's founder, Kanmo, showed him a translation of a poem. This poem, which I here call "November 3rd," impressed him, since it was unlike any other Japanese poem he had read; it was full of quiet humility. Mrs. Imamura, we assume, also told him that the poet who wrote it was famous as a devout Buddhist. It is characteristic of Snyder, then, that despite his strong interest in Buddhism, he did not include the homiletic "November 3rd" in his selection of eighteen poems, focusing instead on pieces vividly describing the poet's close interactions with nature.[2]

By the time Snyder worked on Kenji's poems, four different sets of Kenji's *zenshū,* or complete works, had been compiled and published, ranging from three volumes (1934–1935) to six (1956–1958) — a remarkable development, given that Kenji died in 1933 as basically a single-volume poet. It was not that, as the popular story has it, he was "almost totally unknown as a poet during his lifetime."[3] In fact, his

The first edition of
Spring & Asura, published
in April 1924.

book, *Haru to shura (Spring & Asura),* which appeared in April 1924, electrified several of the poets who read it. The Dadaist Tsuji Jun, the first to review it in a daily newspaper (in July of that year), declared that if he could take only one volume to the Japan Alps that summer, he would favor *Spring & Asura* over *Thus Spake Zarathustra.* In the fall the anarchist Kusano Shimpei, reading it in Guangdong, where he was studying, wrote that he was "shocked" by it and ranked Kenji alongside Carl Sandburg *(Smoke and Steel)* and the Cubist painter-poet Murayama Kaita as the three poets who inspired him. Satō Sōnosuke, who wrote poems influenced by ideas of democracy deriving from the writings of Walt Whitman and of Whitman's English disciple Edward Carpenter, became the first to review it in a poetry magazine (in December) and wrote that it "astonished [him] the most" out of all the books of poems he had received, noting that Kenji "wrote poems with meteorology, mineralogy, botany, and geology." Two years later Shimpei added: "If there is a genius in Japan's poetic world today, I would say Miyazawa Kenji is that honored 'genius.' Even among the leading poets of the world, he emanates an absolutely extraordinary light."

In 1934, a year after Kenji's death, Takamura Kōtarō, a remarkable presence as a painter, sculptor, art critic, and poet, invoked Cézanne in Aix in a commemorative magazine special: "Cézanne had no thought of achieving something new and simply followed the natural road of painting itself; in fact, he tended to lament his lack of ability. Yet the work of this old man in the countryside was so advanced as to give an important clue to the new art of the world, because he had an artistic cosmos stored deeply inside himself and constantly, fiercely dashed toward it. Someone who has a cosmos within himself escapes a locality no matter where he may be in the world, no matter at which periphery he may be. . . . Miyazawa Kenji, the poet of Hanamaki, Iwate Prefecture, was one of the rare possessors of such a cosmos."[4]

Yet it is also true that Kenji died largely unknown. A few poets praising a fellow poet, however extravagantly, does not make him well known, well read. So when the first of Kenji's *zenshū* got under way, in 1934, the Dadaist poet Nakahara Chūya, "an admirer over a decade," wondered: "Has he not been recognized until this late date because there was insufficient advertisement? Because he did not live in Tokyo? Because, other than being a poet, he had a profession, that is, a teaching profession? Because he had no communication with the so-called literary establishment? Or because of a combination of these things?"[5] The answer to the last question is yes, though we must add one more factor, the obvious one that *Spring & Asura* was the only book of poems that Kenji published.

FAMILY AFFLUENCE AND BUDDHISM

Miyazawa Kenji was born on August 27, 1896, in Hanamaki, Hinuki County, Iwate Prefecture, in the Tōhoku (northeast) region of Japan. At that time Hanamaki was a small town with a population of about 3,000. The Sino-Japanese War, Japan's first imperialistic military venture since the country terminated its isolationist policy in the middle of the century, had ended the previous year. Both Kenji's father, Masajirō, then twenty-two, and his mother, Ichi, nineteen, came from mercantile families named Miyazawa. Though unrelated, the two families were regarded as branches of the same *maki,* or "bloodline" — a word suggesting in the Tōhoku dialect not just a familial group that was wealthy and therefore greedy but, more insidiously, one accursed with one of the diseases thought incurable, such as leprosy and tuber-culosis.[6] Miyazawa Kenji, who contracted tuberculosis in his early twenties, ended up living with both stigmas.

Masajirō's father, Kisuke, ran a pawnshop and dealt in secondhand goods, especially clothes. He did a particularly booming business with the laborers who flooded into the region when the railways were extended north through Iwate to Aomori during the first phase of Japan's rapid modernization effort; the construction ended in 1891. Ichi's father, Zenji, did even better. His holdings in timberland were so great, it was said, that you could walk straight to the neighboring prefecture to the west, Akita, without once leaving the forests he owned. He helped to found a bank, to develop the area's hot springs into what might today be called a theme park, and to build a local light railway line that would play an important role in Kenji's imagi-nation. Called the Iwate Keiben Tetsudō, it originated in Hanamaki and extended east, toward the port town of Kamaishi on the Pacific coast.

In his business endeavors Masajirō emulated Kisuke and Zenji. He inherited Kisuke's trade, but, not content to be just a retailer, he be-came a wholesaler of secondhand clothes — which were in fact clothes left unsold and discounted. He traveled as far as Kansai and Shikoku to stock his inventory. (Zenji's investments in forests extended to Shi-koku.) He also profited from wars, especially the First World War, in which Japan mainly played a profiteering, bystander's role and saw its economy more than triple. He had a talent for stocks. In the fall of 1918 Kenji wrote to his closest friend, Hosaka Kanai, that Masajirō's assets based on his stock holdings would grow, "on their own," to be large enough for the family "not to have to trouble others even if [Kenji's] parents became ill for the rest of their lives."[7]

In his old age Masajirō boasted, "Had I not known Buddhism, I'd have been able to build a fortune as great as Mitsui's and Mitsubishi's." More than a touch of exaggeration no doubt, but when Kenji described himself as part of a local *zaibatsu,* in 1932, a year before his death, he was basically telling the truth. In responding to a writer who had apparently solicited comments on a children's story, Kenji said: "I've ended up writing these worthless things [suggestions] because you said I was too self-deprecating. . . . After all, I am linked to what is called a *zaibatsu,* a social defendant,[8] in my home region, and if anything happens that makes me stand out, there is always more resentment than anything else, which I truly hate. I've experienced many things that I truly hate."[9]

The family's affluence explains why Kenji was able to spend his entire salary at the Hinuki (later, Hanamaki) Agricultural School on costly "modern" things from Tokyo, such as foreign-language books, Western records (Beethoven, Tchaikovsky, Bach), and Western nude paintings (reproductions, one assumes), as well as one thousand (!) *shunga,* or erotic prints. Indeed, it was while he was at school that he began collecting records, in the end making himself Hanamaki's greatest record collector. He sometimes paid poor students' travel expenses and at times treated his entire class to a meal at an expensive restaurant.

Buddhism permeated the Miyazawa household. Masajirō was an earnest follower of the school of Buddhism known as Jōdo Shinshū (True Pure Land). When he was twenty-four, he started a study group with his friends and invited religious scholars and leaders to lecture. His children attended many study group sessions. He bought Buddhist books and to house them built a small library in his garden, where everyone was free to read them. As one anecdote has it, his second son, Seiroku, when three or four, visited his maternal grand-mother, Saki, and was served some cookies. He would not touch them, saying: "These would create *bonnō* in me." *Bonnō*, or "hindrances," is an all-encompassing term for anything that leads you astray and deters you from becoming "awakened," including food that whets the appetite. Saki was amused: "This kid talks like an old man!"

Among the Buddhist texts Kenji grew up listening to are the *Shōshin nembutsu ge*, "Hymn to *Nembutsu* as True Faith," also known as *Shōshinge*, by Shinran (1173–1262), who founded the Jōdo Shinshū, and the *Hakkotsu no go-bunshō*, "Holy Words on White Bones," by Rennyo (1415–1499), who revived the school two centuries later. The former is a 120-line verse equating *nembutsu*, the prayer saying "Praise to Amida Buddha," with faith, and the latter is a short homily on the transience of life, hence the importance of conversion to the Amida faith at the earliest age. One famous sentence in "Holy Words" is "You have a ruddy face in the morning and find yourself turned into white bones in the evening." It is said that Masajirō's older sister, Yagi, whose first marriage had failed and who was living in her brother's house when her nephew was young, recited the "Holy Words" for Kenji in lieu of lullabies.

Of these two works, the hymn may have given Kenji the earliest familiarity with Japanese verse. Though composed in classical Chinese, each line with seven characters, it is read and recited in a Japanized pronunciation of Chinese in such a way that most lines come out in seven-five, or twelve, syllables, thereby creating the same rhythm as the verseform of *wasan*. *Wasan* are Japanese Buddhist hymns that repeat the same syllabic pattern of seven and five, which is basic, even exclusive, to Japanese versification. In view of the great differences between Chinese and Japanese, Shinran surely pulled off a neat linguistic sleight of hand in this composition.

In 1911 Kenji attended a summer Buddhist lecture series run by the scholar-priest Shimaji Taitō. One important subject covered by the series was the *Tannishō (A Record in Lament of Divergences)*, a collection of Shinran's words. In November 1912, in a letter to his father, Kenji declared: "I have made the first page of the *Tannishō* my entire religion." But did he have in mind section 1 or 3? The former asserts that the moment you think of saying a *nembutsu* your salvation is assured, and the latter contains Shinran's most famous words: "Even a good person goes to the Pure Land; how couldn't an evil person?" — a postulate that reversed that of his teacher and founder of the Jōdo-shū, Hōnen (1133–1212): "Even a criminal is reborn in the Pure Land; how, how on earth, can't a good person!"[10]

CONVERSION TO THE NICHIREN-SHŪ

In September 1914, when he was eighteen, Kenji was "extraordinarily moved" to read Shimaji Taitō's just-published Chinese-Japanese edition of the Lotus Sutra. Though Shimaji was of the Jōdo Shinshū, a relatively unaggressive school of Buddhism, the reading led to Kenji's conversion to the radical Nichiren-shū (Nichirenism) and then to the ultranationalistic Kokuchūkai (the Pillar of the Nation Society). The Nichiren-shū was founded by Nichiren (1222–1282), a firebrand who equated faith in the teachings he thought he found in the Lotus Sutra with national salvation, and the Kokuchūkai by Tanaka Chigaku, in 1914, to propagate militant interpretations of Nichiren's teachings, as if Nichiren himself wasn't militant enough.

The Kokuchūkai, which today promotes such benign matters as closer relations with Korea, in the 1920s and 1930s spearheaded the kind of Nichirenism that could easily skew the course of the nation. Tanaka advocated *tengyō*, "heaven's task," which may be called Japan's answer to America's manifest destiny, and defined his society's duty as achieving a "spiritual unity" throughout the world with "Japan as the Imperial Headquarters and the Japanese as soldiers."[11] Among his ardent admirers in the military was Ishihara Kanji, mastermind of the Manchurian Incident in 1931, which led to the establishment of the new state of Manchukuo and marked the start of what some would later call Japan's "Fifteen-Year War." For a while Inoue Akira (or Nisshō), leader of the Blood League that assassinated a former minister of finance, the head of Mitsui in 1932, thought of joining Tanaka's group. Among the more prominent Nichiren followers was Kita Ikki, who was executed as philosophical leader of the 2/26 (February 26) Incident of 1936, an attempted coup d'état in which the lord keeper of the privy seal, the minister of finance, and the inspector-general of military education were assassinated. The suppression of the rebels allowed the hard-liners in the army to consolidate their power.[12]

Kenji knew none of these men. But decades later his faith in the Nichiren-shū and his association with the Kokuchūkai would provoke the question: Had he not died in the early 1930s, would he have joined the ranks of the chauvinistic militarists? After all, did he not call Nichiren "the world's one and only teacher" at the end of 1920, and, on joining the Kokuchūkai later that year, did he not write, "I only exist within Teacher Tanaka Chigaku's command," adding, "If so ordered, I'll go anywhere, be it the Siberian tundra or Inland China"?[13] We must also consider Miyazawa's notions of war and world order. From his religious perspective the world was in the Final-Days-of-the-Dharma phase, as Miyazawa told his father in a letter of March 1918, and from the perspective of global politics, "war constantly occurs as a result of overpopulation and [the need for] adjustment to it."[14] By then the First World War was winding down, but despite President Woodrow Wilson's talk of a "war to end all wars," some of the Allies were readying to move against Russia's revolutionary government. Japan and Britain landed their forces in Vladivostok in April, the prelude to a large-scale Siberian invasion. The military, if not militarism, was a fact of life, explaining frequent references to the military in Kenji's stories and plays, if not in his poems.

So one might ask: What drove Kenji to such radicalism or at least to a school of religion that took such a radical stance? Except for a brief period when he tried to convert his father, engaging in a violent argument, wasn't Kenji by all accounts a benign, pleasant, "Buddha-like" person? Kenji did not leave a body of writings on religion so we can only speculate, but I think that there were basically three reasons for Kenji's conversion. One was the secularization of the Jōdo Shin-shū, which, in his eyes, made it too lax, too cavalier, to deserve being called a religion. Another was a combination of circumstances that did not allow him to settle for easy compromises. And a third was his conflict with his father.

To begin with the last reason, Kenji's father was the kind of man who would harp on the fact that he had permanently damaged his intestines when he contracted dysentery from Kenji while nursing him when the boy, at age six, was quarantined with the disease. After his son's posthumous fame was secured, he ostentatiously converted to the Nichiren-shū, even though he had scornfully rejected it when his son tried to convert him. Kenji did not leave any overt complaint about him, but in an early tanka he recorded his discomfort with his father's petit bourgeois manner:

Father father why in front of the superintendent did you wind your
large silver watch?

Kenji wrote this cutting piece in April 1909, on the day he entered the Morioka Junior High School and was taken to its dormitory with

Masajirō. The playwright and biographer Aoe Shunjirō was probably right in condemning Masajirō as an "utterly intolerable small-scale philistine." Aoe was from the Tōhoku, where he witnessed firsthand many instances of stifling father-son conflict, and he wrote that it was particularly difficult for a first son to escape his merchant father's grip.[15]

Worse still was Masajirō's business of pawnbroking and selling used clothing. Serving as storekeeper, as he often did, Kenji had to keep his "feelings . . . locked up in a gray stone box," as he wrote to Hosaka in early 1920, for otherwise he'd find himself in "an environment in which [he] wouldn't be able to read a single page of a book." Kenji went on to characterize that environment with these words: "old cotton for futon, *grimy* cold children's clothing, blackish pawned goods, a frozen store curtain, blue envy, desiccated calculation, and others."[16] In the summer he wrote Hosaka again, reporting that lately he had been "bad-tempered and easily becoming furious":

> Anger flares up and my body feels as though it has entered alcohol. Sitting at a desk and remembering someone saying something, I suddenly feel like smashing the desk with my whole body. Anger looks red. When it's too strong the light of anger becomes so luxuriant it rather feels like water. In the end it looks deathly pale. To be sure, anger doesn't make you feel bad. . . . This paroxysm that almost turns me into a madman I mechanically call up by its true name and join my hands. An asura in the world of humans becoming a buddha. And filled with joy I turn the pages again.[17]

So here we have Kenji's first image of himself as an asura. As he proclaims in the title poem of *Spring & Asura:*

> how bitter, how blue is the anger!
> At the bottom of the light in April's atmospheric strata,
> spitting, gnashing, pacing back and forth,
> I am Asura incarnate[18]

Kenji evidently regarded his image of himself as an asura to be so true that he used *Spring & Asura* as the title not just of his first collection of poems, which was published during his lifetime, but also of the two subsequent collections that were not. So what is an asura?

In one Buddhist scheme, there are "six realms" in this world, and these are inhabited by unenlightened beings, all subject to rebirth, which are, in ascending order, hell dwellers, unsatiated spirits, beasts, asuras, humans, and heavenly beings. In the glossary of his Chinese-Japanese edition of the Lotus Sutra, Shimaji Taitō defines asura: "'Ashura' *(asura),* also abbreviated to *shura.* . . .

A sculpture of an eighth-century asura at the Kōfukuji Temple, Nara.

They are said to be *akushin* [evil deities or spirits] fond of fighting and quarrels who are constantly at war with various heavenly beings and who live, in a number of phases, under the mountains or at the bottom of the ocean." In the Buddhism-permeated Japanese imagination, indeed, the word *shura* or *ashura* — *asura* is Sanskrit — readily evokes the image of bloody fights or fighters, or a state of fury. And for Kenji, his "fundamental intuition" was that the real world is the realm of asura, a realm full of killing and conflict, as the philosopher Umehara Takeshi points out.[19] Or, as the Buddhist scholar Gene Reeves put it, Kenji's was a "radical affirmation of the reality and importance of this world . . . in which suffering has to be endured."[20] The saving grace, as it were, is the Buddhist teaching that every being could be succored, "an asura in the world of humans becoming a buddha."

Ōtani Kōzui, the head of the dominant branch of the Jōdo Shinshū, the Nishi-Honganji, was an adventuresome, enterprising man. From 1902 to 1903, he led an expedition to Ceylon, India, and Tibet to collect ancient Buddhist texts and artifacts, the first such attempt by a Japanese group.[21] His father had begun the new era of Meiji (1868–1912) with radical reform and modernization in mind, with an emphasis, a few decades into the era, on efforts to counter Christianity, which, owing to waves of Westernization, had found a growing number of converts among young men and women. These efforts worked so well that by the end of Meiji the school's annual budget is said to have exceeded that of Kyoto City. In 1908 Kōzui built an extravagant villa-cum-museum-cum-school on Mt. Rokkō, in Kobe, complete with a mile-long cable car reaching from the seashore to the building, as well as telescopes and searchlights — all brand-new Western equipment seldom seen in Japan at the time. In 1914 he went bankrupt and, with other scandals breaking out, was forced to resign the post of head of the Jōdo Shinshū. We can well imagine that Kenji was so chagrined by such developments he eagerly sought another Buddhist school that advocated more pristine, vigorous goals.[22] As one result Kenji turned to vegetarianism. In May 1918, in a letter to Hosaka, he described his aversion to eating the "bodies of living things" in graphic terms:

> In spring I stopped eating the bodies of living things. Nonetheless, the other day I ate several slices of tuna sashimi as a form of *magic* to "undertake" my "communication" with "society." I also stirred a cup of *chawanmushi*[23] with a spoon. If the fish, while being eaten, had stood behind me and watched, what would he have thought? "I gave up my only life and this person is eating my body as if it were

something distasteful." "He's eating me in anger." "He's eating me out of desperation." "He's thinking of me and, while quietly savoring my fat with his tongue, praying, 'Fish, you will come with me as my companion some day, won't you?'" "Damn! He's eating my body!" Well, different fish would have had different thoughts. . . .

Suppose I were the fish, and suppose that not only I were being eaten but my father were being eaten, my mother were being eaten, and my sister were also being eaten. And suppose I were behind the people eating us, watching. "Oh, look, that man has torn apart my sibling with chopsticks. Talking to the person next to him, he swallowed her, thinking nothing of it. Just a few minutes ago her body was lying there, cold. Now she must be disintegrating in a pitch-dark place under the influence of mysterious enzymes. Our entire family has given up our precious lives that we value, we've sacrificed them, but we haven't won a thimbleful of pity from these people."

I must have been once a fish that was eaten.[24]

That the Jōdo Shinshū's practice of eating fish, poultry, and meat turned Kenji off became clear in "The Great Vegetarian Festival," a story he wrote just a few years before his death. It takes the form of a report on an international gathering of vegetarians that was supposed to have taken place in a village near Trinity Harbor, Newfoundland. In this festival, the opponents, mainly represented by the Chicago Cattle Raisers Association, are fully allowed to air their views — a wonderful setup for reminding us that practically all the arguments for including meat in the diet and for eating vegetables only were current in the 1920s. The climax comes when the last speaker, a self-styled "follower of the Honganji Branch enlightened by the incarnation of Amida Buddha Shinran," argues: "This world is one of suffering; there is not a single thing done in this world that is not suffering; this world is all contradictions; it is all sins and crimes. . . .

What we perceive as justice is in the end no more than what feels nice to us. . . . [In the circumstances we can only] leave ourselves to the Enlightened One and Savior toward the West, Amida Buddha, so we may liberate ourselves from the contradictions of this world. Only then things like vegetarianism will be all right," and so forth.

It is when he goes on to say that Sakyamuni "allowed the eating of animal meat obtained by deeds that are not too cruel. . . . In his last years, as his thought became ever more round and ripe, he seems not to have been a total vegetarian" that the narrator forgets his reporter's role, leaping to the podium and arguing:

> Buddhism's starting point is that all living things, we who are so full of pain and sadness, together with all these living things, want to liberate ourselves from this state of pain. . . . All living things have been repeating transmigration for immeasurable *kalpa*. . . . Sometimes a soul perceives itself as a human. At other times it is born in a beast, that is, what we call an animal. . . . As a result, the living things around us are all our parents and children, brothers and sisters, as they have been for a long time. People of different religions will think this idea too serious and terrifying. [Indeed] this is a serious world to a terrifying degree.[25]

This argument wins the day for the vegetarians, though Kenji closes the story by pointing out it has all been "fantasy." But his aversion to eating the "bodies of living things" was so strong that he even felt guilty eating vegetables.

IWATE AND KENJI AS A STUDENT OF AGRICULTURE

The Iwate that inspired and distressed Kenji was prone to natural disasters. In 1896 alone, the year Kenji was born, the region was hit by a 125-foot-high tsunami, which killed 18,000 people in the prefecture, on June 15; by a flood following a heavy rain, on June 21; by an earth-quake, on August 31, which destroyed a great many houses; and by another flood, on September 6, which raised by fifteen feet the level of the Kitakami River, the main drainage system that runs through Iwate. It was in fact partly because of the August 31 earthquake that the Miyazawas were able to pinpoint the date of Kenji's birth: it struck four days after he was born, remembered Ichi, who had covered her baby with her own body to protect him. For some reason, Kenji routinely gave his date of birth as August 1.

Historically Iwate was also prone to famine. Occupying the northern part of the main island of Honshū, the Tōhoku faces the Pacific Ocean at a point where the cold current Oyashio, which flows southwest along the Chishima (Kurile) Archipelago, turns east as it meets the warm Tsushima Current, which flows from the west into the Pacific through the Tsugaru Strait. Whenever one of the two prongs of the Oyashio extends too far south and overwhelms the Tsushima Current, cold descends on the region and crop failure results. During the Edo Period (1603–1868), Iwate was hit by a major crop failure every sixteen years on average, each time killing tens of thousands of people. The region was once called the "earth of white bones" and later "Japan's Tibet."

The frequency of crop failures increased during Kenji's lifetime. Major ones occurred in 1902, 1905, 1913, 1926, 1929, and 1931. By the early twentieth century the central government was able to prevent most outright deaths from starvation, but crop failures ravaged rural areas. One consequence was rampant human trade: people selling their young daughters to brothels. It was illegal but openly, and widely, practiced. Prostitutes are a haunting presence in Kenji's poems, though not in the ones I have translated. "A Record of Food in a Mountain Village," a poem by Mori Saichi, a reporter for the *Iwate*

Daily, written in 1929, details another consequence. That year, like the previous one, had experienced drought, the one in 1928 devastating dry-land rice and vegetables. Describing a family of nine, "four above fifteen years old, five below," in Yamane Village, Kunohe County, Iwate, Mori mainly listed what the family ate from August 24 to 30. The measuring unit *shō* is about 3.8 pints, *gō* one-tenth of it. Nuts of the Japanese oak *(nara)* or acorns, along with horse chestnuts, or conkers, were important food during famines:

> 24th: 1 *gō* of millet, 5 *gō* of wheat, and 2 *gō* of *menoko* (powdered sea-weed): morning, pickled cucumbers, cowpea soup; noon, same as morning; evening, wheat gruel, bean paste (licked)
>
> 25th: 1 *gō* of millet, 5 *gō* of soybean: morning, pickled cucumber, cowpea soup; noon, sweet potatoes steamed in a pan, bean paste; evening, millet gruel, pickled cucumber
>
> 26th: 7 *gō* of millet, 5 *gō* of wheat, 1 *shō* of nuts of Japanese oak trees: morning, nuts of Japanese oak trees, millet gruel, pickled cucumber; noon, same as morning; evening, wheat gruel, corn steamed in a pan, pickled *nappa*.[26]

The crop failure that struck a year after Kenji's death was the worst on record. Some historians say that it directly led to the 2/26 Incident of 1936 mentioned above. The revolting officers and the fifteen hundred soldiers who followed them were mostly from peasant families in the Tōhoku. The manifesto of the revolt spoke of "rampant greed" at the top that thrust "millions of people ... into insufferable pain."

Calls for radical agricultural reform were inevitable as modern scientific knowledge advanced. One might say that these began with the idea of abandoning agriculture altogether put forward by Nitobe Inazō, of *Bushidō* fame, in 1898, followed by a range of proposals, though none of them was taken up exactly as advanced.[27] Still, when the Nippon Railway, a company set up to build a railroad through the Tōhoku, completed its ten years of work in 1891, its president, Ono Gishin, decided to commemorate the occasion by creating Japan's first corporate farm in a barren area about ten miles northwest of Morioka, then Iwate's only city. Called Koiwai Farm, it was a Western transplant, complete with silos. Kenji was enchanted by what must have struck him as an apparition in the midst of nowhere. Many of his pieces were inspired by the farm, among them his longest poem, a nine-part, 827-line description of what he saw and thought as he walked from a train station to the farm.[28]

Iwate Prefecture expressed its own concern through various measures. It established agricultural stations, one for Hinuki County in Hanamaki in 1897. It also founded the Morioka Higher School for Agriculture and Forestry, in 1903, the first of its kind in Japan. It was the latter's agriculture department that Kenji entered, in April 1915. Masajirō probably chose the school for Kenji, but agriculture, along with the range of subjects the field covered, apparently suited Kenji's interest and inclinations, for it set his course.[29] The dean of the department, Seki Toyotarō, who was awarded a doctorate for his study of volcanic ash that turned into soil, was an eccentric—he famously lectured with his face turned sideways, without looking at his students—but Kenji got on very well with him and thrived under his tutelage. Kenji's graduation paper was on the "value of inorganic elements in the humus for plants," a controversial issue at the time, as Kenji called it. It consisted of assessments of soils from four areas in Iwate with generally negative conclusions. At Seki's request, Kenji stayed on at the higher school—today's equivalent of college—as a researcher of geology, pedology, and fertilizers. His first assignment, which started in April 1918, was to map soils in Hinuki and was financed by the county. In May Seki arranged to commission him as "assistant in experiment guidance." He wanted to guarantee Kenji's position, with a plan to recommend his eventual promotion to assistant professorship.

But at the end of June Kenji was diagnosed with pleurisy. Pleurisy — lung apex, bronchial infection, and pneumonia, to add the names he listed in a letter to a friend in October 1932 — was often equated with tuberculosis. A family with a member suffering from TB was shunned, if not ostracized, so it was necessary to camouflage the disease. Kenji's mother, Ichi, had TB; so did her sister, Koto. Kenji sensed the true nature of what he had, and as he went home to rest on July 4, he predicted to a friend that he would live for only another fifteen years. This prediction proved to be uncannily accurate. The first time around he recovered after a dozen days, but the disease kept recurring, at times severely, until his death exactly fifteen years later.

On July 20 he resumed work, but on August 24 resigned the researcher's post, though he continued soil mapping until the end of September. For his work he had to carry a good deal of equipment, along with samples, which often included rocks he had collected, his hobby since a boy. It was during this period that he became aware of his physical limitations. "I can't do anything. I plow the land but I plow two *tsubo* [four square yards] and I rest and rest without interruption. I handle something a little heavy and I have a spell of cerebral anemia," he wrote to Hosaka in October.[30]

KENJI AS TEACHER OF AGRICULTURE

That same month Kenji's beloved sister Toshiko, a student at Japan Women's College in Tokyo, fell ill; in December Kenji, told of her hospitalization, went to Tokyo with his mother. That year the Spanish flu raged, and the family learned that it was, in fact, the direct cause of Toshiko's illness. But it was the bronchial infection she had developed along with the flu that would lead to her death from TB four years later. Kenji tended to her in the hospital every day and filed reports on day-to-day developments with Masajirō. At the end of February Toshiko had recovered enough to be able to leave the hospital, and in early March Kenji brought her back to Hanamaki. Thereafter at times she felt well enough to be up and doing things, such as attending lectures on dressmaking and making clean copies of Kenji's tanka, and in September 1920 she took on the job of teaching English and home economics at her alma mater, Hanamaki Middle School for Girls. But her recovery proved deceptive. In August 1921 she vomited blood and had to resign. The news prompted Kenji to return from Tokyo, where he had gone to escape Masajirō and to join the Kokuchūkai and where — after Takachio Chiyō, Tanaka's top aide, persuaded him to focus on his work rather than become a proselytizing member as Kenji had wanted — he was making a paltry living mimeographing. That period, which lasted for seven months, was to be the only time when Kenji managed to live more or less apart from his father.

Kenji, who had graduated from the agricultural school with today's equivalent of a master's degree in May 1920 — his final report for Hinuki County was "Geography and Geology" — became a teacher at the Hinuki County Agricultural School in December 1921. Created in 1907 to teach sericulture, the school had broadened its scope that year. When Kenji, who had given a series of lectures on mineralogy, soils, chemistry, and fertilizers there in 1919, arrived to take up the teaching post, the school was as it had been originally: a humble establishment with thatched roofs. In fact, Kenji's business-man uncle was working to build new buildings for the school at the time. Introduced by the principal to the students, Kenji simply said, "I am Miyazawa Kenji, just introduced," and stepped down from the podium. He had a buzz cut and wore a Western suit with high collar, a point worth noting if only because he had worn formal Japanese at-tire when he had earlier given lectures at the school.

The year 1922 opened with Kenji writing a string of poems that would form *Spring & Asura,* beginning with "Refractive Index." It is said that one inspiration behind Kenji's sudden ease in turning out free verse was a music teacher at Toshiko's school — though by the time Kenji visited him there and the two quickly had become friends, Toshiko had left. "Love and Fever" is the first poem expressing Kenji's concern for Toshiko. In April, when the ceremony to welcome newly enrolled students was held, Kenji was assigned to teach alge-bra, English, fertilizers, agricultural production, produce, meteorol-ogy, chemistry, and soils, in addition to giving practical training in growing rice in paddies. On April 8, the day after the ceremony, he wrote "Spring & Asura." Some commentators find it significant that April 8 is the Buddha's birthday. With six teachers in all, including the principal, taking care of just two classes, four were idle when two were in class. The abundance of time and the liberty he enjoyed must have added to the surge in Kenji's creative energy.

While at the school Kenji also wrote a dozen songs and plays for his students. He composed the music for the songs as well, and he made sure that his students sang them when he took them to other schools, with himself serving as conductor. The earliest play he wrote at the school was probably the one staged in March 1922. It described the crown prince of England, who was scheduled to visit Japan the

Miyazawa Kenji in front of a blackboard at the Hinuki County
Agricultural School, ca. 1922. Photograph © Rinpoo.

following month. As the student who played the prince's role recalled,
it depicted the prince meeting Japanese people of all classes, calling
those who were deferentially speaking to him in English (perhaps)
"fools" to their faces, while returning polite greetings to those rude
fellows who, assuming that he did not understand Japanese, said in-
sulting things to his face. The play was an uproarious success. When
the school in the new buildings opened as Hanamaki Agricultural
School, in April 1923, two of Kenji's plays, *Shokubutsu ishi* (The plant
doctor) and *Kiga jin'ei* (The starvation camp) were staged to mark the
occasion. The first pokes fun at someone who makes money by pre-
tending to know everything about plants, and the second mocks the

military, which is unable to procure enough food for the rank and file. Both plays are slapstick.

In July 1922 Toshiko was moved to the family's "other house" in Shimoneko, since her mother had become worn out looking after her.[31] Toshiko was provided with a nurse and two maids, and her sister Shige made meals for them. Kenji visited her every day. In early November, her condition worsening, she was brought back to the Miyazawa house, and on November 27 she died. Kenji shouted *daimoku* — the Nichiren-shū prayer *Namu Myōhō Renge-kyō,* "Praise to the Sutra of the Lotus Flower of the Wonderful Dharma" — into her ear before she died. It was sleeting that day. "The Morning of Last Farewell," "Pine Needles," and "Voiceless Grief" all describe the occasion. The following summer Kenji went to visit Karafuto, the southern half of Sakhalin, which became Japanese territory in 1875, on the pretext of asking one of his classmates, now with the company Ōji Paper, to consider two of his students for employment. Unable to shake off his grief, he wrote a series of elegies for his sister. Except for the poems Takamura Kōtarō wrote about his wife, Chieko, who suffered from schizophrenia and died in a mental hospital, there is nothing comparable in Japanese poetry to these and other poems about Toshiko.[32]

In December 1924 Kenji published his book of children's stories, *Chūmon no Ōi Ryōriten (A Restaurant with Many Orders).* As he had with *Spring & Asura,* he printed a thousand copies at his own expense.

KENJI THE "REAL PEASANT"

As he told a visiting teacher in the summer of 1923, Kenji liked teaching. He said the secret lay in arousing interest in one's students and not paying much attention to textbooks, heresy in the days when strict adherence to textbooks was de rigueur. His casual dress and his unorthodox behavior — he liked to exit the classroom through the window — delighted his students as much as his kindness attracted them. For a while Kenji even grew his hair long and used pomade. Still, he left the school in the spring of 1926. He wanted to become a "real peasant." As early as April 1925 he wrote one of the students he had successfully placed with Ōji Paper, "I can't continue indefinitely doing lukewarm things like teaching that's going nowhere, so probably next spring I'll quit to become a real peasant. And I think I'd create a farmer's theatrical troupe regardless of profit or loss."[33] In June he put it more poetically, if you will, in his letter to Hosaka (in which he used no punctuation):

> Next spring I will quit teaching and become a real peasant and
> work Out of various bitter hardships I foresee things like burrs
> of blue vegetables and flashes of poplars I have changed quite a
> bit from what I was in the Morioka days In those days I was only
> thinking of a flow of water like transparent cold water nymphs but
> now I pray for rice seedlings beds and faintly muddy warm water
> by a grass-growing dam in which many microorganisms pleasantly
> flow my feet dunked in it my arms dunked in it myself repairing
> the water outlet.[34]

Kenji's decision to become a "real peasant" and to do something useful for the peasantry came partly from what he observed daily. He wrote in the proem to his second, unpublished, *Spring & Asura:*

> I received such relaxing, solid status [at school].
> Nevertheless, in time,
> I gradually became used to it
> and calculated somewhat excessively the number of kimonos every
>   child had
> and the amount of protein every child took at every meal.

One incident that graphically revealed the inadequate protein intake among ordinary villagers occurred during the 1926 ceremony of the National Foundation Day, on February 11. A student fainted, and Kenji rushed to him. He had vomited *daikon kate,* finely sliced daikon often added to meals to increase their volume.

At that time there was also a growing sense that a proper person could not ignore the plight of workers and peasants. The establishment of the Soviet Union gave momentum to the proletarian movement, which conversely fanned the government's fear of anything smacking of communism, socialism, or liberalism. In March 1920 Japan's stock market crash, comparable to Wall Street's nine years later, occurred and the economy dipped and bobbed, hardly moving thereafter. Social unrest grew. One of the worst manifestations of that unrest was the murder of many Koreans and Chinese following the great September 1923 earthquake. This violence was partly caused by the rumor that they were responsible for the natural disaster that had killed 100,000 people and rendered 1,000,000 homeless.

In 1924 the education ministry banned the staging of plays in schools. In March 1925 the Public Safety Preservation Law passed the Diet, and it went into effect the next month. Declaring that any attempt to change the *kokutai,* national polity, as well as any attempt to deny the sanctity of private property was equally punishable by law, it would become the government's most powerful weapon for suppressing freedom and dissent. Between 1922 and 1926, the home ministry expanded the Special Higher Police, the thought police, and set up its branches in nine prefectures.

Conscious of his "idle rich" status, Kenji was sympathetic to the proletarian movement. Though in the end he would decide that the kind of revolution advocated by the communists was not for Japan, at one point he helped the Hinuki-area branch of the Labor and Farmer Party, which was under close police surveillance. His idea of promoting *nōmin geijutsu,* agrarian art, came out of that sympathy. To do so on his own terms, he had to become independent of the education system that was being quickly hemmed in. But that idea would prove too dangerous.

Kenji in work clothes at his Shimoneko house, 1926.

Not that the idea of "agrarian art" itself was radical or dangerous. Iwate's board of education and its league of agricultural societies established a "citizens' higher school" — a lecture series for adults — and ran it at Hanamaki Agricultural School during the first three months of 1926, after Kenji firmed up his decision to quit and before he actually had. Among its stated purposes was to improve the conditions of "the villages that are in the extremely worrisome state of utter fatigue" and to "advance rural art *(nōson geijutsu)*." Kenji was one of the two dozen lecturers lined up for the program, and he gave a total of eleven lectures focusing on agrarian art.

On April 1, 1926, Kenji left his family home to live alone in the "other house," the one in which Toshiko had spent her last months. He did not do it on the spur of the moment. He had employed two carpenters to renovate the house in mid-January, and he did the interiors himself, in Constructivist mode. His move hardly went unnoticed. Kenji was, after all, the first son of an important man of Hanamaki. The morning edition of the *Iwate Daily* summarized

Kenji's remarks on the previous day — the day he resigned from the Hanamaki Agricultural School:

It seems to me that villages are certainly at a dead end economically and in various other ways. I'd like to do a bit of research on the "village economy," which I am short of [don't know much about], at some university in Tokyo or Sendai. And for about half a year I'd like to engage in tilling here in Hanamaki and lead my life, that is, a life of art. So I will hold things like a magic-lantern gathering every week and hope to give a record concert once a month. Fortunately there are about twenty comrades, and my plan is to exchange the produce I have made with effort, with sweat on my brow, and go on to live a quiet life.[35]

What he actually did was to set up a society to educate the farmers — "We are all farmers," he declared — and for that purpose he prepared an "outline for agrarian art." Named Rasu Chijin Kyōkai, the Society of Rasu Earthmen,[36] the society seems to have come into being in late August 1926, as Kenji worked out the "outline" and managed to give a few lectures. But with a well-meaning write-up in the *Iwate Daily* on February 1, 1927 — Kenji was again identified as the first son of Miyazawa Masajirō, of Hanamaki, even though he was a thirty-year-old man with a pedagogic career behind him — the thought police made an overt move to look into Kenji's activities as potentially socialist. Kenji wilted, and the society practically stopped functioning. It ceased to exist in August 1928 when a high fever felled Kenji.

Kenji meticulously went about the preparation of the outline, which was based on his lectures of early 1926. First he itemized the topics he would address:

Introduction
   . . . What we together are to discuss from now on . . .
Rise of Agrarian Art
   . . . Why our Art must rise now . . .

Essence of Agrarian Art

  ... What makes up the heart of our Art ...

Fields of Agrarian Art

  ... How they can be categorized ...

Isms of Agrarian Art

  ... What kinds of argument are possible in them ...

Production of Agrarian Art

  ... How we can begin work, how we should proceed ...

Producer of Agrarian Art

  ... What the artist means in us ...

Criticism of Agrarian Art

  ... How a correct evaluation and appreciation is first made ...

Synthesis of Agrarian Art

  ... Oh friends, let us combine our righteous strengths together so we may turn all our countryside and all of our lives into a large single four-dimensional art ...

Conclusion

  ⊙ What we need is the transparent will and the large power and heat that wrap the Galaxy

Kenji then lined up his thoughts on each topic. Among the ones he included in the introduction, "What we together are to discuss from now on," for example, are:

We are all farmers. We are extremely busy and our work is hard.

We'd like to find a way to lead a brighter, livelier life.

Among our ancient masters there were often people who did.

We'd like to discuss this matter in the unity of the proofs of modern sciences, the experiments of the seekers of the way, and our intuitions.

Unless the entire world becomes happy, there can be no happiness for individuals.

The consciousness of the self gradually evolves from individuals to groups to societies to the Universe.[37]

He then set out to write detailed lecture notes for each such thought, but he apparently managed to do so for just one topic, "Rise of Agrarian Art," either because he ran out of time or because he lost courage somewhere along the way. Still, a look at the writers and thinkers he cites reveals a good deal about the tenor of Kenji's reading and sentiments at the time. They were Büchner (most likely the German materialist philosopher Ludwig Büchner, 1824–1899, rather than his writer brother, Georg, 1813–37) on the changing economy and the advancement of "ownership impulse"; Daniel Defoe on his idea of the circulatory relationship between food and labor; Oscar Wilde for his observation on living and being merely alive;[38] William Morris for his statement "Art is man's expression of his joy in labour"; Leo Tolstoy for his thought that only 10 percent of the population "buy and enjoy" games, while 90 percent work themselves to death; Oswald Spengler on the decline of art, "music since Wagner, painting since Manet and Cézanne," and so on; Ralph Waldo Emerson on the decline of creativity and the withering of the roots of beauty; Romain Rolland on "unproductive pleasures"; Ōtani Kōzui — the only Japanese person who appears — for his observation cited with apparent incredulity, "Some call themselves thinkers; but is there anyone who has no thought?"; Edward Carpenter; and Leon Trotsky. The last name serves as a reminder that Kenji had *Das Kapital* among his books and once asked a friend to lecture on Lenin's treatise *The State and Revolution*. In any event, he guarded these notes and showed them to no one except perhaps to some of his close comrades.

Kenji tilled the land as he said he would. He had to clear a plot of sandy land atop a cliff rising from the Kitakami River. Though an inveterate walker and a good mountain climber when a little younger, he wasn't really cut out for that kind of labor. He tired easily. To live like a regular peasant, he insisted on subsistence food, rejecting, for example, the lunch boxes his mother made and brought. He ate mainly the vegetables he grew. Among them was the tomato, an imported species then still regarded as an herb because of its strong smell. Some of the people who visited Kenji or worked with him during that time came away with the indelible memory of eating tomatoes, sometimes only that. Kenji owned only two rice bowls and a set of chopsticks for kitchenware. One of his aunts remembered telling him once to eat more nutritious things. His response was, "I like eggplants, and I need nothing else as long as I have them. I eat five or six of them. But one day I said to a neighborhood child, 'I've just eaten two eggplants.' He was shocked and said, *You ate as many as two!*"

Not that Kenji could not afford adequate food, or anything else he might have needed. He could obtain from Masajirō any amount of money he wanted, as he did, for example, when he went to Tokyo in December that year to study a variety of things in the shortest possible time: Esperanto, typing, the organ, and cello. He attended lectures such as the one given by the Finnish minister, who spoke in Japanese about the need to abandon materialistic culture to build a new agrarian culture. He unthinkingly went there poorly dressed, to find himself the only sartorially deficient one in the well-dressed crowd. But he was also the only one to have a lively conversation with the diplomat on the subject he had discussed, asking him about things like the position of dialects in the culture to be newly promoted. Tōhoku dialects are only too famous for their unintelligibility to outsiders; Kenji once wrote a tanka in Iwate dialect and translated it into standard Japanese for Hosaka. During this trip he also went to see Takamura Kōtarō, the only established poet he would meet and talk to in his lifetime.

Kenji's life as a peasant at the Shimoneko house was full of incongruities. For example, not just the Ponderosa tomato but also the flowers in his garden were grown from the seeds he ordered from the

Yokohama branch of the English purveyor, Sutton & Co., an extravagant thing to do. He held record concerts as well as live concerts with his comrades, with himself playing the organ or the cello, both expensive instruments. While refusing to eat proper food, he used a *rear cart* (the English name was used then, as it is today) to carry things — a two-wheeled vehicle originally designed to be pulled by a bicycle but more often pulled by hand in Japan. The erudite popular writer Inoue Hisashi, who says he was inspired to become a writer when he read Miyazawa's writings, with their singular use of onomatopoeia, has depicted the poignancy of the incongruities Kenji created for himself:

> Kenji loved rubber boots, but no peasant in those days wore such high-quality things. Everyone knitted his own heel-less straw sandals and went to the paddies and walked in the fields in them. Kenji, incidentally, was undexterous, I gather. While studying at the Morioka Higher School he had to knit straw sandals in practical training, but he didn't know where to stop so would end up making sandals longer than the abacus. No matter how often he tried, the result was the same.
>
> According to the testimony of his students, Kenji always used socks. The heels became holes, so this aspiring farmer wore them with the torn parts up. Even so, there was not a single peasant in the Tōhoku region in those days who wore socks. Even in the dead of winter they usually went about barefoot, wearing *tabi* only for the first three days of the New Year or for the ceremonies of marriage and funerals.
>
> He sometimes went to town to sell the vegetables grown in his field, loading them on a rear cart. Now, of course you can't possibly expect the scion of a distinguished family of Hanamaki to walk about, loudly calling out his wares. He simply pulled his rear cart along, smiling, so most of his stuff would end up unsold. Then, as he went home, this brand-new peasant would give away his vegetables to any passerby who cared to take them. That's strange, too. No peasant gives away his produce, free. If you can't sell your stuff, you exchange it for something else to get value out of it. I'd say that is the Peasant's Way.

Above all, to go about pulling a rear cart was beyond belief. In Hana-maki in those days there were only a few mercantile houses owning one, and having one meant a big house. It would be comparable to today's Mercedes-Benz, and you couldn't use such a thing selling vegetables.

Kenji liked uniforms. He once designed what he called "farm-work clothes," which resemble today's work clothes, and had the design printed in the bulletin of the Iwate Prefectural Farm Association. He wasn't satisfied just designing them; he apparently had one set made for himself and proudly wore it, looking triumphant as he pulled his rear cart hither and thither. The Hanamaki people seem to have been aston-ished by this, too.[39]

"Astonished" is putting it kindly. Kenji provoked ridicule, envy, and resentment among the *real* peasants, as he chronicled in many of the poems in the third, unpublished, *Spring & Asura*. It did not help that the Shimoneko district included Dōshin-chō. During the Toku-gawa Period *dōshin* were a low stratum of policemen (but still samu-rai) and, following the custom of the period that based residential zoning on profession, they lived in the section named after them. With the arrival of the Meiji Era and the abolition of the samurai class, many low-ranking samurai like these willy-nilly became peas-ants, an outcome that intensified their ancestral discontent and dis-gruntlement. The Teikichi in the poem "In Dōshin-chō toward day-break" was one of that lineage.

From the spring of 1927 Kenji increasingly turned his attention to devising "fertilizer plans" for the farmers. These plans required de-tailed knowledge of the place: the type of paddy, distance from the river, the kinds of grass or weed that normally grow, soil permeabil-ity, and so forth. Here is the beginning of a poem in which Kenji de-scribes how he determined a fertilizer plan through an imagined (perhaps actual) series of questions:

Well then, let's calculate.
The place is in Kamineko, Yuguchi, correct?
What you got there,
what's the total size of it?
5 tan 8 se, you say.
Is that on the book,
or by the unit of 100 harvested bundles?
Is it a paddy always dry or moist?
Then, how many steps up from the river?
You mean, it's on the same level
as the Kannon-dō where there's that chestnut tree, isn't it?
Oh, I see, it's just below it.
And it's still a step up
from the river, isn't it?
Does trefoil clover grow
on and around the ridges?

And here is an example: the plan he prepared for a Takahashi Hisanojō on February 5, 1932 (1 *kan* = 8.27 pounds):

Dear Sir,
I have consulted your thoughts and made calculations as follows:

manure	200 *kan*
ammonia sulfate	2 *kan*
fish lees	3.5 *kan*
soybean waste	10 *kan*
strong perphosphoric acid	4.5 *kan*
bone meal (steamed)	2 *kan*
carbonated lime (2 millimeter)	7.5 *kan*

In Akashibu use 2 *kan* of ammohos instead of ammonia sulfate and [decrease] the perphosphoric acid to 3 *kan*.

Next, last year's aluminum phosphate was evidently effective. This is because you should not overlook that the fact that you had 3 *koku* and 70 percent of fourth-class rice means that phosphoric acid, which has gradual effect, worked extremely well.

Except that the above [aluminum phosphate] hates to be used in consecutive years, so I have selected bone meal this year; as for sulfate of potash I've decided to let lime work on the manure and have taken it out as you wished.

This letter's postscript details the rising prices of rice and fertilizers, as well as the wage hikes laborers were demanding, concluding that the kind of discount Takahashi had requested on lime would be difficult to give. Among other things, the letter suggests that Kenji's fertilizer plans failed to produce desired results from time to time and, when they failed, elicited complaints from their users.[40] In fact, some disappointed farmers are known to have threatened him, forcing Masajirō to pay for the "losses."

LAST YEARS

In June 1928, to explore money-making ventures for Masajirō, Kenji went to Sendai, then to Tokyo, where he saw an exhibition of ukiyo-e, or woodblock prints, an important event in his visit to the metropolis. The show, held in a museum in Ueno Park, featured fifty-three prints by Kiyonaga, 147 by Utamaro, and nineteen by Harunobu. Kenji also went to Ōshima to advise Itō Shichio, who planned to set up an agricultural school on that island. Without telling Kenji, Itō had wanted to arrange a marriage for him to his sister, Chie. Nothing came of it. But the trip did produce two series of poems. "Impressions of a Floating-World Paintings Exhibition" is one of the nine Kenji set aside under the heading "Tokyo."

That summer drought set in after torrential rains, and crop failures were expected. Kenji ran about helping the farmers. In August he came down with a cold, and the resulting fever lasted for forty days. He was diagnosed with infiltration of both lungs. He had to leave the

Shimoneko house to be cared for in his family home and never got another chance to live in the house where he had tried to create an agrarian culture. Masajirō may have decided that it would reflect poorly on him if he left his first son in a quarantine house.

In early 1930 Kenji had a remission. He became a little hopeful and began to grow vegetables and flowers in the garden. In the meantime, fear of the thought police may have taken its toll on him. Writing in March to a former student who was later a member of his society, he said, "There [at the Shimoneko house] it was as if I were ill (both in mind and body) almost from beginning to end, and I am very sorry about it." In contrast, he fondly remembered the school where he had taught. About the same time he wrote another former student, now a schoolteacher, that the "four years at the agricultural school were the time most worth my effort" and the "peak of my life." This letter also shows the kind of fear people had of TB — the same kind of fear that AIDS, much later, initially provoked. In telling his correspondent that he was separately sending him a book on how to play the organ, he took care to note: "I haven't touched it since I became ill, and in the end I didn't get tuberculosis, but just in case I have fully disinfected it so you may use it without worry."[41]

A year earlier, an entrepreneur with an ambition to ameliorate the difficulties of farm life had visited Kenji for advice on his business. His name was Suzuki Tōzō. Suzuki, the son of a peasant, had grown up poor and had written two books, one scientific, one utopian, on the elimination of poverty, and he had started a small firm to pulverize limestone for fertilizer. He had succeeded in securing Koiwai Farm as a customer but was stalled in finding other volume buyers. Then he heard that Miyazawa Kenji was known as a "deity of fertilizers." By then Kenji had prepared fertilizer plans for a great many farmers — by the end of his life some two thousand of them, all free of charge.

Suzuki's visit eventually led to Kenji's agreement, in February 1931, to work for his firm, Tōhoku Rock-Crushing Company, as an "engineer" — or, as Kenji explained to Seki Toyotarō, his former teacher who was now consultant to the National Agricultural Research Institute in Tokyo, as an "advisor tasked with product improvement and research, preparation of advertisement copy, and promotion and explanation."

Masajirō, concerned about his son's career, "invested" five hundred yen in Suzuki's firm. Suzuki, overjoyed, promised Kenji an annual salary of six hundred yen. At the time the daily wage for a laborer was half a yen, so it may seem a fairly good salary, except that it came with a proviso: that it be paid in pulverized rock. Kenji was torn. The work was to improve agriculture, but it was a money-making enterprise, extracting pennies from hard-pressed peasants. He also knew it was a losing proposition. Competition was fierce, and Suzuki's factory did not have the machinery to pulverize limestone to the desired fineness. Nonetheless, he realized it was his last chance to prove himself to Masajirō. He worked hard — most of the one hundred letters that survive from spring to the end of that year are business letters addressed to Suzuki — and won a great deal of business.

The work, which required him to travel constantly, did not take long to bring him down. On September 20, when he arrived in Tokyo lugging a large trunk heavy with samples of lime, he was feverish. Kenji took to his bed as soon as he reached an inn. He was convinced he was about to die. The following day he wrote a brief letter to his parents and another to his siblings. In the former he said: "All my life you have bestowed on me the kind of considerateness that no child anywhere could expect to receive, but I have always been selfish and have ended up like this. In this life I have been unable to repay the smallest fraction of your considerateness; I only pray to definitely

Kenji's 1933 drawing of his niece Fuji, whom he describes in "October 20th."

return it in my next life and in the life after it."[42]

At the end of the month Masajirō arranged to have him transported home in a sleeping car. It was during that fall that Kenji scribbled the poem "November 3rd" in a pocket notebook. Two weeks before that, he had written the poem "October 20th." The three-year-old girl described in the latter is Fuji, the daughter born on February 15, 1929, to Kenji's youngest sister, Kuni.

During the next two years, Kenji felt a bit better at times, but he knew he would not recover. He wrote letters, responding to requests from Suzuki Tōzō and, when asked, preparing fertilizer plans. One remarkable creative effort he made during this period was the writing and revising of *bungoshi,* to be discussed in greater detail below. Just as remarkable, he kept writing poems closely describing what it felt like to be ill — poems about hallucinating, dreaming, listening to his heartbeat. Among the poetry files left was *Shitchū* (During illness), a collection of such pieces.

In the final days of his life, he spoke of his writings to three different people in three different ways. He said to Ichi: "In these children's stories I wrote out the blessed teachings of the buddhas as best I could. So, some day, I'm sure everyone will be delighted to read them." To Masajirō, he said, "Please dispose of these manuscripts as you see fit; they are the traces of my misguided thoughts." To his brother, Seiroku, he said, "I'll give you all my manuscripts. If some publisher comes to you with an offer to publish them, let them, no matter how small the house. If no one does, don't bother."[43]

During the three days of the local shrine festival, from September 17 to 19, which features the deer dance, Kenji came down from his room on the second floor to watch the festivities at the storefront, at times walking to the gate. It happened to be a year of bumper crops, and each town created a fanciful festival cart, some of them fifty feet high. On September 20 Kenji's condition took a sudden turn for the worse. A doctor from Hanamaki Hospital diagnosed acute pneumonia. Kenji and Masajirō talked about the last days of Shinran and Nichiren. Kenji then took up a brush and wrote two tanka on a sheet of paper. Lately he'd been practicing calligraphy.

Within these ten square miles: is this in Hinuki alone?
The rice ripe and for three festival days
            the whole sky clear

Because of an illness, crumbling,
            this life —
if I could give it for the dharma
            how glad I would be

At about seven that evening a farmer came for advice on fertilizers. Kenji changed to proper attire, came down from the second floor, sat formally in the foyer, and listened to the visitor's prolix explanations. The interview lasted almost an hour, worrying and exasperating the family members within hearing distance.

At about eleven-thirty the following morning, the family heard Kenji loudly reciting *Namu Myōhō Renga-kyō*. They rushed upstairs. He had vomited blood and was deathly pale. He requested that

Masajirō print a thousand copies of a Japanese translation of the Lotus Sutra and distribute them. Kenji died, shortly afterward, at 1:30 P.M.

Miyazawa Kenji began writing just about the time the movement called *genbun-itchi,* meaning "unity in speech and writing" — a shift from *bungo,* "literary language," to *kōgo,* "colloquial or spoken language" — was ending. In his comprehensive survey of the movement's effect on poetry writing, the poet and educator Hitomi Enkichi (1883–1974) traces the origins of the movement to the proposal submitted, in 1867, to the last shogun, that the use of Chinese characters in Japanese be abolished, and ends his account as the Meiji Era (1868–1912) draws to a close.[44] The result of the struggle to adopt a new mode of writing — part of the worldwide phenomenon that Jerome Rothenberg and Pierre Joris call "persistent thrusts to raise demotic, colloquial, common speech as the language of a new poetry and culture"[45] — was transformative. In verse, the effort began with experiments in being more flexible than was possible with the almost exclusive verseforms till then — the five-seven-five-seven-seven-syllable tanka, *kanshi* (verse in classical Chinese), and the five-seven-five-syllable haiku (called *hokku* until about 1900) — and was complete with a rapid acceptance of free verse. One outcome was a total disregard for syllabic count among some haiku poets and, somewhat later, among some tanka poets as well. One tanka poet who directly influenced Kenji is Ishikawa Takuboku, who lineated tanka — an extraordinary break with the tradition of writing tanka in one line.[46] Kenji followed the practice with much greater freedom: while Takuboku limited himself to breaking his tanka into three lines, Kenji broke his into two to six.[47]

The acceptance of free verse was so rapid that by the early 1910s Yamamura Bochō, to name another poet who is thought to have influenced Kenji, joined a group calling itself Jiyūshi-sha, the Free Verse Society, in 1910, and was soon writing poems such as "Tawagoto" (Jibberish), which simply juxtaposes each legally defined crime with a random object:

larceny goldfish
robbery bugle
extortion Chinese fiddle
gambling cat
fraud calico
bribery velvet
adultery apple

and so forth. Bochō is especially known for a visual poem, "Fūkei" (Landscape), with the subtitle "pure-silver mosaic": a painterly depiction of a whole field of rapeseed flowers through the exclusive use of the hiragana syllabary, each line fitted with nine characters. Kenji also tried to create visual effects in a number of poems.

The period was marked by a "flood of translations of Western literature and an invasion of daily language by scientific (technical) terminology," as the erudite critic Katō Shūichi, a hematologist by profession, sums it up in his concise history of Japanese literature.[48] No one who was educated could remain immune. Kenji, who pursued agriculture in college, delighted in sprinkling his poems with exact technical terms, even using words whose origins are hard to pin down. Among the latter is the term *shinshō*, the idea of which, along with *mental sketch* (in Kenji's English), guided all of his writing, as he explains in the proem to *Spring & Asura*. (There it first appears in the phrase *shinshō sketch,* then as an independent word. In the title poem it appears in the first line.) But is it a Japanese translation of the English *image* or of the German *Bild*? Did Kenji get it from Henri-Louis Bergson? From Tagore's *Gitanjali*? From Mallarmé? Or is it a word he coined from Buddhism, which holds that all phenomena are derived from the mind? As the Kegon-kyō or Avatamsaka-sutra states, "In all the three worlds there is only this one mind."[49]

Kenji also loved concocting foreign-sounding words for his stories. His indulgence in this practice drew utter contempt from the one person who counted in the field of children's stories in those days: Suzuki Miekichi. In 1918 Miekichi started a magazine dedicated to the genre, called *Red Bird,* with quite a lineup of endorsers among the literary luminaries of the time. In 1925 Kikuchi Chūji, who illustrated *A Restaurant with Many Orders,* sent a copy of the book to Miekichi and, when he was in Tokyo, went to see him with a new story of Kenji's. As he recalled, Miekichi said to him: "Sir, you know I am an Imperial Loyalist and patriot. You better take a manuscript like this to Russia or something."[50] Miekichi's secretary, Nomachi Teiko, remembered Kenji himself coming to see Miekichi. After he left, she recalled Miekichi saying, "To be sure, his work is different, and the amusing bits are amusing, but as children's reading materials go, it just does not fit *Red Bird.*"[51]

One word coined by Kenji has endured: *Iihatov,* a name he made up for "Iwate Prefecture, Japan." In a leaflet for *A Restaurant with Many Orders,* he suggested that it may be situated "in the fields which Little Claus and Big Claus used to till, in the same world as the looking-glass country the little girl Alice traipsed through, far northeast of the Tepantar Desert, way east of Ivan's Kingdom," adding it exists in "the author's *shinshō.* . . . Everything is possible there. In a flash you may leap onto an ice cloud and travel north followed by the jet stream or talk to an ant waking under a red flower petal." Today Iihatov is a nickname of Iwate, but as to its origins, you can only say that it may be a combination of some Esperanto sounds and the German *Ich weiß nicht wo* (I don't know where).

The acceptance of free verse did not mean the automatic abandonment of traditional forms. In Japan, the continuing popularity of tanka and haiku to this day amply attests to this. Nor did it mean a simple abnegation of "literary language" and syllabic patterns or *teikei,* set forms. The genre of *bungo-teikei-shi,* literary-language poems in set forms (often simply called *bungoshi*), lived on for a few decades. Kenji, who began by writing tanka, himself continued to write *bungoshi* after moving on to *kōgo jiyūshi,* free verse in colloquial language (today simply called *shi*), the genre for which he is justly famous. (By definition, standard tanka and haiku are *bungoshi,* although in the odd Japanese world of specialization, neither tanka nor haiku are included in the category of *shi.* Kenji himself made this distinction, preparing separate files for tanka, which he called *kakō,* "tanka manuscripts.")

The lack of a clear break was to be expected. Aside from the strong appeal of set forms, free verse confronted poets, as it still does, with the question of what exactly constitutes a poem. Among other poets, Hagiwara Sakutarō, whose first book, *Tsuki ni hoeru (Howling at the Moon),* published in 1917, was acclaimed as "epochal" in the development of colloquial free verse, wrestled with the question throughout his life as a poet, in the end concluding that the tanka might be the ideal verseform for the Japanese language. It was the verseform in which he, too, had started out as a poet. In his waning years Sakutarō also "retreated" to the use of literary language.[52] Kenji, unlike Sakutarō, did not leave a mass of writings on poetry and poetics, and his free verse does not normally give the impression that he contended with the question of what makes a poem. On the contrary, the first feeling a reader is likely to come away with is that Kenji "dashed off" his poems. As Katō Shūichi has observed,

> the first characteristic [of Kenji's poetry] is the torrent of excited words that swallow up dialects, onomatopoeias, Buddhist terms, scientific terms, and all, a kind of garrulity that spews out of the poet's insides. The objects these words wake up are fresh and clear, and the echoes of these words stay in your inner ear. There probably is no other poet who has managed to create such a poetic effect with such abundant vocabulary. The second characteristic is the grand expansion of his imagination. . . . Miyazawa Kenji liberated his imagination toward the Galactic universe.[53]

Kenji himself insisted that his pieces were "no more than coarse and hard *mental sketches* I write down under various conditions while no legitimate study is allowed, as long as circumstances allow, every time I get a chance, in preparation for a certain psychological work," as he wrote to the poet Mori Saichi in February 1925.[54] Among his students at the agricultural school where he taught, he was known to scribble in a pocket notebook whenever words and lines hit him, regardless of time or circumstances.[55] A stray remark of Kenji's one student remembers from the day they climbed a small mountain together may reinforce this impression. Begin a poem with the first impression that flashes in your mind, Kenji advised; he then went on to recite a poem he apparently had composed on the spot.[56]

Furthermore, all the many drafts and rewrites Kenji has left may confirm this view of him as a poet on a linguistic rampage. The huge difference in size between the twelve-volume *zenshū* published at the end of the 1960s — each volume with less than four hundred pages — and the fifteen-volume *zenshū* during the 1970s — most volumes from seven hundred to well over a thousand pages — comes from the simple fact that the latter set out to collate and list all revisions and different drafts that have survived. Indeed, with a number of poems the "final" versions depend on an editorial decision. Yet Kenji's drafts and rewrites also suggest that he had the nagging sense that free verse was too easy — that he struggled to work out poems in a sphere where all the defining constraints on diction and form, let alone content, were lost. That nagging sense may explain the pervasive use of seven- and five-syllable patterns throughout his free verse, often where the reader is likely to miss them because the descriptions are in language that is so close to common speech, although one could also say that those patterns came naturally to him.[57]

Above all, Kenji wrote *bungoshi* even as he wrote free verse — "from 1910 to 1930," as noted on the cover of a loose collection of 112 poems with a notation, "originals [drafts] of *bungoshi* (unfinished)" — that is, almost the entire span of his life as a poet. The last two collections of poems he put together shortly before his death, in 1933, were of "finished" *bungoshi,* one of fifty pieces, the other of one hundred, neither containing repeats of pieces in the loose collection. Other *bungoshi* are scattered throughout his manuscripts. Some of these poems are rewrites of tanka or free verse, some variations on the same themes. As he did with his free verse, he kept revising them. As a result, with many it is possible to follow the process of selection and elimination necessitated by the constraints of set forms. The photograph on page 44 shows a manuscript that in the end produced the

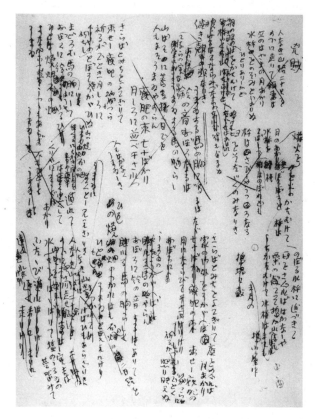

The manuscript of "Tilting," written
toward the end of Kenji's life.

following *bungoshi,* each line with seven-five syllables, though no at-
tempt to reproduce the syllabic count is made in the translation:

> Tilting the flames of moonlight
>> the water-pounder all alone
> pounds truly inedible
>> puckery nuts of oak.

Well then I say and cross the road
      to dozens of bundles of manure.
In the prayerful moon whitening
      I spy a door that's gone to seed.

On a dozing horse's chest
      a blurry bell clunks, trembles.
In the mountain's burnt fields, stony fields,
      fragile people are asleep.

Torizō, who came running all night
      over the mountain's deserted two-day road
chewed on the stalks softened in salt
      and ran away again into the distance.

"NOVEMBER 3RD"

In view of all these factors, especially Kenji's propensity to revise, it is ironic that the poem that rapidly won him nationwide fame, became almost synonymous with his name, and turned him into a "saint" is one that he scribbled in a pocket notebook while ill and probably never thought of revising. That Kenji obviously meant it as a prayer adds some poignancy to the way it was later used for national or nationalistic causes. The piece is usually cited by its first line, *ame ni mo makezu,* though I call it simply "November 3rd," for the date noted at the outset, "11.3" (see photograph). Here are three different translations of the first two lines: *ame ni mo makezu/kaze ni mo makezu,* both in seven syllables.[58] (See pp. 217–20 for two complete translations.)

Bending neither to the rain
Nor to the wind
    — Geoffrey Bownas and Anthony Thwaite

The first two pages of "November 3rd," as written in Kenji's notebook
on November 3, 1931. Photograph © Rinpoo.

Strong in the rain
Strong in the wind
— *Roger Pulvers*

Unbeaten by rain
Unbeaten by wind
— *Katsunori Yamazato*

The story of how "November 3rd" gained prominence is worth
telling in some detail.

In February 1934, five months after Kenji's death, the freshly
formed Society of Friends of Miyazawa Kenji had its first meeting in
the restaurant Mon Ami in Tokyo. Among the twenty-one people at-
tending were the poets Kusano Shimpei, Takamura Kōtarō, and
Nagase Kiyoko. The main attraction at the meeting was a trunkful of

Kenji's manuscripts his brother, Seiroku, had brought for everyone's inspection. "Its voluminousness, the richness of its content . . . overwhelmed those who had gathered," Nagase reported. It was on that occasion that the small "black pocket notebook" was found in a pocket of the trunk.[59] But if "November 3rd" impressed some of those present, it wasn't included in the first attempt at a *zenshū* (in three volumes, October 1934 to October 1935), even though it saw print in the second issue of the Society of Friends' magazine, in June 1935. This suggests that Shimpei and other editors of the *zenshū* didn't think much of it as a poem. Nevertheless, in January 1936 it was picked up in an anthology of modern Japanese poets, then, in July of the same year, in a volume on works by the "people who have exerted themselves for the progress of mankind," one in a literary series for the young.

In 1941 Qian Dao-sun, a professor of literature at Beijing University, translated "November 3rd" into Chinese for inclusion in his anthology of Japanese poetry, ancient and modern. A different translation into Chinese was made, apparently for a book to be disseminated in Manchukuo, the nation Japan established in 1932. In 1942 the cultural division of the Taiseiyokusankai — the government-initiated nationwide patriotic association formed in October 1940 when war with the United States seemed more and more inevitable — included it in an anthology of patriotic poems. On September 20, 1944 — by then Japan's war in the Pacific was becoming desperate — the philosopher Tanikawa Tetsuzō gave a lecture at Tokyo Women's College, titling his talk "Konnichi no kokorogamae," "What we must be prepared to do today." Noting that the date marked the day before Kenji's death eleven years earlier, he said:

I think this poem [*Ame ni mo makezu*] is the most sublime of all the poems the Japanese since Meiji have ever made. There may be more beautiful poems, or deeper poems. But in its spiritual sublimity, I know of no poem comparable to this one. The almost immeasurably great meaning this poem has for this age — which is in the end the meaning the poet called Miyazawa Kenji has for this age — is what I wish to talk about. . . . Since Meiji we have had many great men-of-letters. But I have no one except Kenji before whose grave I wish to genuflect with true humility.[60]

In June 1945, two months before Japan's defeat, Tanikawa's lecture was published as a booklet with the title *Ame ni mo makezu.* Twenty thousand copies were printed, this at a time when paper shortages were so acute that publication of any kind was controlled and when city after city was being incinerated by U.S. bombings. This turn of events created a strong suspicion afterward, unjustly, I think, that Tanikawa was willingly aiding and abetting Japan's militaristic causes. To his credit, Tanikawa did not try to retract or hide what he'd said or done during the war. Instead, he maintained his admiration for Miyazawa Kenji and his poems, especially *Ame ni mo makezu,* to the end of his life. The poet Tanikawa Shuntarō, whose essay, "Four Images," appears in this book, is his son.

The fame of "November 3rd" was considerable by then. The poet Aida Tsunao, who was in Shanghai when Japan surrendered, re-membered writing from memory the entire piece, in brush and ink, on a white wall in his house. He had the "sentimental" thought that some Chinese who could read Japanese might think that some Japanese suffered from a "bad conscience."[61] Some years after the war he wrote "Densetsu" (Legend), a haunting poem based on the rumors he had heard while in China about a great number of people killed in Nanjing at the end of 1937.[62]

Following Japan's defeat in the Second World War, the ministry of education wanted to keep "November 3rd" in a textbook. The idea was to encourage the children living in the war's difficult aftermath to learn the spirit embodied in its opening lines. But the Occupation censors objected. The offending passage was this:

eating one and a half pints of brown rice
and bean paste and a bit of
vegetables a day

The original reads: *ichinichi ni genmai yon gō to on/miso to sukoshi no/yasai o tabe.* The rice part says "4 *gō* of unrefined rice." The censors found the figure given in the passage quoted above unacceptable. When the Occupation-decreed daily ration of rice was 2.1 *gō,* which was a goal mostly unmet in the grave food shortages facing Japan then, and there were reports of people starving to death, 4 *gō* was just too much. In the end the education ministry, with Seiroku's agreement, changed the figure from 4 to 3 and managed to have the poem included in the textbook. As a result, children at many schools were required to chant "November 3rd" in unison, and the failure to do so in accordance with the prescribed manner incurred punishment. In his essay, included in this volume, the poet Yoshimasu Gōzō, who was in grammar school shortly after the war, reminds us of this.

BUDDHISM AND KENJI'S LITERATURE

What did Kenji see in Buddhism, and how was what he saw reflected in his writing? Umehara argues that Kenji absorbed a "worldview," as opposed to a "humanview," from Buddhism. Of the principal currents of Buddhism that emerged during the turmoil of the Kamakura Period (1185–1333), Zen sought to get rid of one's hindrances and the Jōdo Shinshū to save the soul from one's evil self. In that sense, both are attempts to extract homocentric elements from Buddhism. In contrast, from the outset Kenji had nothing to do with this "homocentricism, which modern Japanese writers and thinkers, almost without exception, have espoused," says Umehara. The homocentric view meshed with Western humanism, which came into Japan during the Meiji Era. In contrast, Kenji "saw in Buddhism a grand view of the world that is consistent with the findings of modern science," and he spells this out in the proem to *Spring & Asura*. As Umehara paraphrases it,

> the world is a single living life, a single consciousness. This living world splinters into endless diversities, changes multifariously, and becomes changeful lives. Sun and moon, mountain and river, grass and tree, birds, fish, and humans — all these are no more than various manifestations of a single life. And they all turn on and off. Our own lives, like the lives of various other living things, burn fleetingly in a corner of the cosmos. These are lives that turn on and off momentarily but they too are all manifestations of the endless life.[63]

Nearly half a century earlier, the historian of Japanese religion Masaharu Anesaki had made much the same point in summarizing the Kegon-kyō: "The aim of the Buddhist religion . . . is to dispel the illusion of the separate ego and therefore to restore everyone's consciousness to fundamental communion with Buddha and through him with all other beings."[64] And he too felt that this concept went beyond the standard notion of religion; he pointed to Buddhism's "similarities with Leibniz's monadology," a word scarcely remembered now but well known at the time.[65] Kenji himself used the word *monad* often enough in his poems, along with the Buddhist term *mijin,* the smallest unit of matter, which he equated with the atom, that is supposed to be only visible to celestial beings and bodhisattvas.[66]

In "this view of life" — Darwin's phrase from the conclusion of *The Origin of Species* — the essence Miyazawa Kenji grasped was also the central tenet of Mahayana Buddhism: joy in all living things, all phenomena, the conviction that each of them is capable of becoming a buddha. One happily imagines Kenji, having taken to heart the moving last paragraph of Darwin's book, going about in communion with "endless forms most beautiful and most wonderful."

About the Lotus Sutra specifically, Reeves suggests that Kenji absorbed from it the joy of storytelling, the freedom of letting his imagination fly, and a great sense of drama. The literary critic and poet Yoshimoto Takaaki put it this way:

Kenji's drawing of an owl; Kenji did many drawings and paintings throughout his life.

> The largest of the charms that Miyazawa Kenji's works proudly scatter about is the extraordinarily free positioning of the eyes. The eyes in his work, like the ones attached to a giant body that reaches the highest stratum of a skyscraper, capture us in a close-up from an infinite distance. While you are thinking that, the next instant, like the eyes attached to the minuscule head of a crawling worm, they minimize themselves. These eyes even make us feel that they know very well the perspectives with which we are instinctively not familiar and catch us there. Also, we often run into pieces that appear to depict the illusions of the body in which the writer finds his body transformed into a wiggling, crawling worm or partially bloated.[67]

Indeed, much of what Kenji produced is different from what one might expect from someone writing "religious literature." Takachio Chiyō, of the Kokuchūkai, seemed bemused when informed that Kenji had written, in the notebook with "November 3rd" scribbled in it, that *he* had prompted him to the "writing of Lotus Sutra literature *(Hokke bungaku no sōsaku)*." Takachio remembered meeting Kenji in early 1921 and, on learning that Kenji wanted to become a proselytizing member of the society, telling him instead to devote himself to whatever his profession may be, be it the plow, the abacus, or the pen, for that was the true "Hokke training." The advice plunged Kenji into a period of furious writing, enabling him to produce a string of stories.

But Takachio knew none of the effects of his words. When told that he was the impetus for Kenji's religious literature, he reflected: "When people speak of Hokke literature, they seem to refer to poems and stories in praise of the Lotus Sutra or tales of benefits the Buddha brings to people *(rishō-tan)*. . . . In Kenji's case, there are of course some like those, but I think, rather, that he, as a writer with true faith in the Lotus Sutra, called Hokke literature the art that he expressed as irrepressible manifestations of that faith."[68]

Miyazawa Kenji continues to fascinate. In 1995, when an exhibition to mark the hundredth anniversary of his birth was mounted, scholars and writers were invited to discuss him not just as a poet and storyteller but also from the perspectives of dramaturgy, religion, philosophy, semiotics, cosmology, depth psychology, chemistry, and music. The most recent *zenshū,* which started publication that year, is the ninth and encompasses eighteen volumes — a treatment no other Japanese poet of the twentieth century has been accorded. Books and articles about him pour forth unabated.

The core of the fascination is simple: Kenji inhabited both religious and scientific realms. His imagination could fly with metaphysical speculations, while his eyes remained firmly fixed on the physical details of this world. He was endowed with a hallucinatory sensibility and a heightened sense of drama and humor. These traits, when combined with the double vision of religion and science, gave dimension and depth to his writings, whether they dealt with everyday scenes or with the difficulties he faced daily — with himself, with the farmers he tried to help. It is hoped that the selection that follows, which represents about a seventh of Kenji's poems, will open the door to the world he created.

NOTES

1 Here I am following the Japanese custom of referring to certain well-known writers and artists by personal name.

2 On Snyder and Kenji, see Katsunori Yamazato, "Establishing a Sense of Place: A Comparative Study of Two Ecopoets, Miyazawa Kenji and Gary Snyder," *Tamkang Review* 34, no. 3–4 (2004): 113–27, and Ryo Imamura, "Four Decades with Gary Snyder," in *Gary Snyder: Dimensions of a Life,* ed. Jon Halper (San Francisco: Sierra Club Books, 1991), 299–301. For Snyder's translations, see Snyder, *The Back Country* (New York: New Directions, 1967), 115–28.

3 Makoto Ueda, *Modern Japanese Writers and the Nature of Literature* (Palo Alto: Stanford University Press, 1983), 184.

4 All the reviews and comments quoted here are assembled in volume 15 of the *Kōhon zenshū* (Chikuma Shobō, 1973–1977). Tsuji, 1079–80, Satō, 1081–82, Kusano, 1088, 1093–1100. For Kusano, see also the 1977 *Eureka* special, 13–21; Takamura, vol. 8, *Takamura Kōtarō zenshū* (Chikuma Shobō, 1958), 228.

5 Shichōsha, *Gendaishi tokuhon* 12 (1979): 254. The early accolades by Dadaists obviously left the impression that Kenji was one of them. Writing to a friend that he had just finished reading volume 11 of the second Kenji *zenshū* in January 1941, Mishima Yukio (1925–1970) said: "I have deeply felt his greatness and thought of the cheerfulness of Japan's Dadaism." *Jūdai shokan-shū* (Shinchōsha, 1999), 17.

6 Aoe Shunjirō, *Miyazawa Kenji: Shura ni ikiru* (Kōdansha, 1974), 8–10.

7 *Kōhon zenshū,* vol. 13, 106. All Kenji's surviving letters, including those undated, about five hundred in all, are collected in this volume. The letter quoted from here is no. 92, tentatively dated October 1918.

8 *Shakaiteki hikoku.* The idea that being wealthy is a crime and that therefore a

member of the wealthy family is a "social defendant" probably comes from so-cialist ideas. The term sounds translated.

9   Kōhon zenshū, vol. 13, 402. Letter no. 421.

10 Ōhashi Shunnō, ed., Hōnen shōnin eden, jō (Iwanami, 2002), 218. Masaharu Ane-saki, History of Japanese Religion (1928; repr., North Clarendon, VT: Tuttle, 1963), 182–83. One is reminded of the Christian tenet that "prayer is religion in act" (in Auguste Sebatier's words) and of the Christian idea of "justifying sinners" (in Martin Luther's words). William James, The Varieties of Religious Experience, in William James: Writings 1902–1910 (Library of America, 1987), 416 and 225–26. In the Lotus Sutra, the importance of a simple invocation appears in chap. 2, "Skillful Means": "If anyone, even while distracted,/Enters a stupa or mau-soleum/And even once exclaims 'Hail to the Buddha,'/They will have taken the Buddha way" (Gene Reeves, unpublished translation). See also Selected Writings of Nichiren, ed. Philip B. Yampolsky (Columbia University Press, 1990), 308–11.

11 Yoshida Tsukasa, Miyazawa Kenji satsujin jiken (Ōta Shuppan, 1997), 115.

12 Yoshida cogently makes this point in Miyazawa Kenji, 111–28.

13 Kōhon zenshū, vol. 13, 193. Letter no. 177.

14 Kōhon zenshū, vol. 13, 50–51. Letter no. 48.

15 Aoe, Miyazawa Kenji, 28–31, 64.

16 Kōhon zenshū, vol. 13, 177. Letter no. 159.

17 Kōhon zenshū, vol. 13, 184. Letter no. 165.

18 The addition of the word incarnate is my attempt to re-create the assertive tone of the original, which is in seven-five syllables: ore wa hitori no shura nanoda. I seldom make such additions in my translations. Gary Snyder is correct in lit-erally rendering it in his translation as "I am an Ashura!"

19 Umehara Takeshi, "Shura no sekai o koete," in Miyazawa Kenji no shūkyō sekai, ed. Ōshima Hiroyuki (Keisuisha, 1992), 307.

20 Private communication, September 2005.

21 Shimaji Taitō was a member of the expedition. Kenji's poem "Mr. Pamirs the Scholar Takes a Walk" was probably inspired by Shimaji's dignified mien and background.

22 Ueda Tetsu, "'Nōmin geijutsu no ryūsei' ni okeru Kenji no shūkyō hihan," in Miyazawa Kenji no shūkyō sekai, ed. Ōshima Hiroyuki (Keisuisha, 1992), 341–43.

23 Custard with chicken, fish cake, ginkgo nuts, mushrooms, and a few other vegetables, sometimes with shrimp and clams added.

24 *Kōhon zenshū,* vol. 13, 66. Letter no. 63.

25 *Kōhon zenshū,* vol. 8, 241–42.

26 Mori Saichi, *Sanson shokuryō kiroku: Mori Sōichi shishū* (Michitani, 2003), 190–93. The parenthetical additions are Mori's.

27 Nitobe Inazō (1862–1933), agriculturalist, educator, and undersecretary-general of the League of Nations, wrote *Bushidō: The Soul of Japan,* in English, to argue that the samurai lived for ideals as much as knights did. He studied at Johns Hopkins University and married a Quaker, Mary Elkington.

28 The title of this long poem was "Koiwai Farm." For a complete translation, see Hiroaki Sato, *A Future of Ice: Poems and Stories of a Japanese Buddhist, Miyazawa Kenji* (San Francisco: North Point, 1989), 47–71. In his biography, *Hyōden: Miyazawa Kenji* (Ōfūsha, 1968), Sakai Chūichi argues that "Koiwai Farm" follows Beethoven's Sixth Symphony, the "Pastoral," in its structure (159–61). Kenji's students fondly recalled the record concert Kenji held to mark the hundredth anniversary of Beethoven's death (257–58).

29 In his letter to Hosaka in August 1919, written while Kenji was idling, unable to find a job or decide on his future, Kenji says that Masajirō daily lambasted him for doing nothing, though he'd "been to a school of agriculture and forestry in the midst of the suffering of society at large." That year prices, including the price of rice, rose sharply, creating labor disputes and general unrest. In this letter Kenji also relates how he expressed to his father his desire to go to America, which Masajirō dismissed as the "apex of irrelevant notions."

30 *Kōhon zenshū,* vol. 13, 104. Letter no. 92.

31 This house was built expressly for a sick person, a veritable quarantine. Aoe, *Miyazawa Kenji,* 10.

32 Many of them are translated in Hiroaki Sato's *A Brief History of Imbecility* (Honolulu: University of Hawaii Press, 1992).

33 *Kōhon zenshū,* vol. 13, 224. Letter no. 205.

34 *Kōhon zenshū,* vol. 13, 226. Letter no. 207.

35 A summary of remarks, rather than direct quotations, is still the norm in Japanese journalism, and we can't tell which is the reporter's language and which is Kenji's, though "sweat on my brow" seems too glib a phrase for Kenji.

36   Kenji did not explain what he meant by *rasu*. As a consequence, a great many theories have been advanced, ranging from the term being the first part of John Ruskin's name to it coming from a reverse reading of *shu-ra*. See the entry on the society in Hara Shirō, ed., *Miyazawa Kenji goi jiten: Glossary Dictionary of Miyazawa Kenji*. Tokyo Shoten, 1989. In *Miyazawa Kenji,* Aoe points out that *rasu* is the Ainu word for "pine" (138). As for *chijin,* "earthman," the Christian leader Uchimura Kanzō wrote a book called *Chijin-ron,* arguing that Japan's geopolitical role would be as an intermediary between the East and the West — an idea that held sway until well into the Pacific War.

37   *Kōhon zenshū,* vol. 12, bk. 1, 7–9.

38   In his 1891 essay, "The Soul of Man under Socialism," Oscar Wilde wrote, "With the abolition of private property, then, we shall have true, beautiful, healthy individualism. Nobody will waste his life in accumulating things, and the symbols for things. One will live. To live is the rarest thing in the world. Most people exist. That is all." Available at www.wilde.thefreelibrary.com/Soul-of-Man-under-Socialism.

39   Inoue Hisashi, "Kare no yaritakatta koto no risuto," in *Miyazawa Kenji no shūkyō sekai,* ed. Ōshima Hiroyuki (Keisuisha, 1992), 62–63.

40   *Kōhon zenshū,* vol. 13, 387–88. Letter no. 404.

41   *Kōhon zenshū,* vol. 13, 271. Letter no. 258. *Kōhon zenshū,* vol. 13, 271. Letter no. 260. *Kōhon zenshū,* vol. 13, 303. Letter no. 301.

42   *Kōhon zenshū,* vol. 13, 379. Letter no. 393.

43   *Kōhon zenshū,* vol. 14, 715. Entry on September 20, 1933.

44   Hitomi Enkichi, *Kōgo-shi no shiteki kenkyū* (Ōfūsha, 1985). Maejima's proposal is cited on 9–10.

45   Jerome Rothenberg and Pierre Joris, eds., *Poems for the Millennium* (Berkeley and Los Angeles: University of California Press, 1995), 9.

46   Hiroaki Sato, "Forms Transformed: Japanese Verse in English Translation," in *The Poem Behind the Poem,* ed. Frank Stewart (Port Townsend, WA: Copper Canyon Press, 2003), 175–82.

47   Kenji left well over one thousand tanka and lineated a bulk of them when he made clean copies of them. A selection of translations appears in Hiroaki Sato, *Future of Ice,* 5–24.

48   Katō Shūichi, *Nihon bungakushi josetsu, ge* (Chikuma Shobō, 1980), 474.

49 Hajime Nakamura, *Ways of Thinking of Eastern Peoples: India, China, Tibet, Japan* (Honolulu, HI: East-West Center Press, 1964), 353.

50 Sakai, *Hyōden,* 253.

51 L. Halliday Piel, *Constructing the Child: Modern Identity in Japan, 1600–1952* (PhD diss., University of Hawaii, 2006), 41.

52 Hiroaki Sato, *Howling at the Moon: Poems and Prose of Hagiwara Sakutarō* (Los Angeles: Green Integer, 2002), 20 and 41.

53 Katō, *Nihon bungakushi josetsu,* 475.

54 *Kōhon zenshū,* vol. 13, 220. Letter no. 200.

55 William Carlos Williams "was at pains to 'get it down.' On prescription pads, on pieces of newspaper, on scrap paper, he would scribble the lines. Later, in his office located in his home, he would type feverishly." Robert Coles, *That Red Wheelbarrow* (University of Iowa Press, 1988), 317. Allen Ginsberg is famous for his motto "first thought, best thought."

56 Kohara Tadashi, *Geppō, Kōhon zenshū,* vol. 13, 1.

57 In *Modern Japanese Poets and the Nature of Literature* (Palo Alto: Stanford University Press, 1983), Ueda Makoto devotes a sizable part of his discussion of Miyazawa to this aspect of his poetry. See esp. 217–27.

58 Geoffrey Bownas and Anthony Thwaite, eds., *The Penguin Book of Japanese Verse* (Middlesex, Eng.: Penguin, 1964), 201–2; Roger Pulvers, trans., *Kenji Miyazawa: Poems* (Chikuma Shobō, 1997), 204–9. Bilingual edition; Yamazato, "Establishing a Sense of Place," 115.

59 Nagase Kiyoko, *"Kuroi techō" o mitsuketa, Geppō, Kōhon zenshū,* vol. 12.

60 Tanikawa Tetsuzō, *Miyazawa Kenji no sekai* (Hōsei Daigaku Shuppankyoku, 1970), 6, 30. For the history of *Ame ni mo makezu,* see Ogura Toyofumi, *"Ame nimo makezu" shinkō* (Tokyo Sōgensha, 1980), 147–49.

61 Aida Tsunao, "Ame ni mo makezu," Miyazawa special, *Eureka,* September extra, 1977, 138–41.

62 Hiroaki Sato, "Seven Japanese Poets Since the War," *St. Andrews Review* (Fall and Winter 1976): 13–16.

63 Umehara Takeshi, "Miyazawa Kenji to fūshi seishin," in *Gendaishi Tokuhon* (Shichōsha, 1979), 164–65.

64 Or, as Daisetz T. Suzuki puts it in *Zen and Japanese Culture* (Princeton University Press, 1959), the Kegon philosophy holds "the balancing of unity and

multiplicity or, better, the merging of self with others" to be "absolutely neces-
sary to the aesthetic understanding of Nature," 354.

65 Anesaki, *History of Japanese Religion,* 93–94.

66 This is reminiscent of William James's observation that the "Buddhistic system
is atheistic." *Varieties of Religious Experience,* 36.

67 Yoshimoto Takaaki, *Higeki no kaidoku* (Chikuma Shobō, 1979), 211.

68 Takachio Chiyō, "Miyazawa Kenji to Hokke bungaku," in *Miyazawa Kenji no
shūkyō sekai,* ed. Ōshima Hiroyuki (Keisuisha, 1992), 620.

A NOTE ON THE TRANSLATIONS

Unless otherwise noted, all translations from the Japanese are by Hiroaki Sato.

POEMS

from SPRING & ASURA

(FIRST COLLECTION)

PROEM

The phenomenon called "I"
is a blue illumination
of the hypothesized, organic alternating current lamp
(a compound of all transparent ghosts)
a blue illumination
of the karmic alternating current lamp
which flickers busily, busily
with landscapes, with everyone
yet remains lit with such assuredness
(the light persists, the lamp lost)

In the twenty-two months, which I perceive
lie in the direction of the past
I have linked these pieces on paper with mineral ink
(they flicker with me,
  everyone feels them simultaneously)
each a chain of shadow and light,
mental sketches as they are,
which have been kept until now.

About these, the man, the Galaxy, Asura, or the sea urchin,
eating cosmic dust, breathing air or saltwater,
may each think up a fresh ontology,
but any one of them too will be no more than a scene in the mind.
Yet certainly these landscapes recorded here
are as they are recorded;
if they represent nothing, that's the way nothing is;
to some degree this holds true of everyone
(because just as everything is everyone in me,
  so I am everything in everyone)

But while these words, supposed to have been copied correctly
in the accumulation of the vast bright times
of the Cenozoic era and alluvial epoch,
already change their structures and contents
in the light and shadow that's equal to a dot
          (or in Asura's billion years)
the tendency could be there
that both the printer and I
perceive them as unchangeable.
Because, just as we perceive our senses,
landscapes, and personalities,
just as we all merely perceive them,
so the records and histories, or the history of the earth,
together with their various data,
(under the temporal, spatial restrictions of karma)
are no more than what we perceive.
Perhaps, two thousand years from now,
an appropriately different geology may win the time,
apposite evidence may turn up successively from the past,

everyone may think that two thousand years ago
colorless peacocks filled the blue sky,
fresh bachelors of arts may excavate
wonderful fossils somewhere from the glittering frozen nitrogen
at the top stratum of the atmosphere,
or discover in a stratification plane
of Cretaceous sandstone
the enormous footprints of an invisible mankind.

All these propositions are asserted
in the four-dimensional extension
as the attributes of imagination and time.

· 1/20/1924 ·

REFRACTIVE INDEX

When a closer one of Seven Forests
is far brighter than it is in the water
and extremely large
why do I have to tread on a bumpy frozen road,
tread on this bumpy snow,
and hurry myself
like a gloomy letter carrier
        (again Aladdin takes the lamp)
toward the kinky zinc clouds beyond?

· 1/6/1924 ·

TRANSLATED BY GARY SNYDER

THE SNOW ON SADDLE MOUNTAIN

The only thing you can count on
is the snow on the string of Saddle Mountain peaks.[1]
The fields and the woods
look either frowzy or dulled
and you can't count on them at all,
so, although it's really such a yeasty,
blurry blizzard,
the only thing that sends faint hope
is Saddle Mountain
    (this is one old-fashioned religion)

• 1/6/1922 •

THIEF

About when the stars of the Skeleton
    were paling in the dawn:
Striding the crackly glitter
    — frozen mud —
The thief who had just stolen a celadon vase
    from the front of a store
Suddenly stopped those long black legs
Covered his ears with his hands
And listened to the humming of his mind.

• TRANSLATED BY GARY SNYDER •

1. In Japanese Saddle Mountain is Kurakake-yama, a parasitic volcano 2,960 feet high, southeast of Mt. Iwate.

THE THIEF

Under the pale blue constellation, the Skeleton, toward daybreak,
he crosses the irregular reflections in the frozen mud
and steals the one celadon jar
placed outside the store.
Abruptly he stops his long, dark legs,
puts his hands to his ears,
and listens to the music box, the electric poles.

• 3 / 2 / 1 9 2 2 •

LOVE & FEVER

Today my forehead dark,
I can't even look straight at the crows.
My sister, just about now
in a cold gloomy bronze-hued ward,
begins to be burnt by transparent rosy fire.
Truly, though, sister,
today I too feel weighed down, terrible,
so I won't pick up willow flowers and come.

• 3 / 2 0 / 1 9 2 2 •

(mental sketch modified)

Out of the gray steel of imagination
akebi vines entwine the clouds,
wildrose bush, humus marsh
everywhere, everywhere, such designs of arrogance
  (when more busily than noon woodwind music
  amber fragments pour down)
how bitter, how blue is the anger!
At the bottom of the light in April's atmospheric strata,
spitting, gnashing, pacing back and forth,
I am Asura incarnate
  (the landscape sways in my tears)
Shattered clouds to the limit of visibility
  in heaven's sea of splendor
    sacred crystalline winds sweep
      spring's row of *Zypressen*
        absorbs ether, black,
          at its dark feet
            the snow ridge of Tien Shan glitters
              (waves of heat haze & white polarization)
            yet the True Words are lost
          the clouds, torn, fly through the sky.
        Ah, at the bottom of the brilliant April,
      gnashing, burning, going back and forth,
    I am Asura incarnate
      (chalcedonous clouds flow,
        where does he sing, that spring bird?)
    The sun shimmers blue,

Asura and forest, one music,
   and from heaven's bowl that caves in and dazzles,
   throngs of trees like calamites extend,
      branches sadly proliferating
   all landscapes twofold
   treetops faint, and from them
 a crow flashes up
      (when the atmospheric strata become clearer
      & cypresses, hushed, rise in heaven)
Someone coming through the gold of grassland,
someone casually assuming a human form,
in rags & looking at me, a farmer,
does he really see me?
At the bottom of the sea of blinding atmospheric strata
   (the sorrow blue blue and deep)
Zypressen sway gently,
the bird severs the blue sky again
   (the True Words are not here,
   Asura's tears fall on the earth)

As I breathe the sky anew
lungs contract faintly white
(body, scatter in the dust of the sky)
The top of a ginkgo tree glitters again
the *Zypressen* darker
sparks of the clouds pour down.

• 4/8/1922 •

DAYBREAK

The rolling snow
gets bright peach juice poured into it,
the moon left unmelted in the blue sky
purring gently to heaven
drinks once again the diffused light
    (pāra-samgate bodhi svāhā)[2]

SUNLIGHT AND WITHERED GRASS

  From somewhere a chisel stabs
  and a blue haze of light paraffin;
  circling, circling, a crow;
    crow's creak . . . crow tool
(Will this change)
(It will)
(Will this change)
(It will)
(How about this)
(It won't)
(If that's the case, hey, bring here
a bundle of clouds, quick)
(Yes, it will change, it will)

• 4/23/1922 •

2. Part of the last phrase in the Prajnaparamita Hrdaya Sutra (Heart Sutra): "Those who have gone to the other side, enlightenment, be happy."

CLOUD SEMAPHORE

Ah, it's great! clear — clean —
wind blowing
farm tools twinkling
vague mountains
    — lava-plug   magma
all in a dream where there's no time

    when cloud semaphores
    were already hung
    in the stark blue east

the vague mountains . . .
    wild geese will come
      down to the four
        cedars tonight!

• TRANSLATED BY GARY SNYDER •

A BREAK

Up in that gaudy space's
upper section a buttercup is blooming
      (high-class buttercup it is but
      rather than butter, from sulphur and honey)
below that, wild parsley and clover
and a dragonfly of worked tinplate.
rain crackles,
    oriole cries in the

silverberry tree . . .
stretch out on the grass
there's white and black both in the clouds;
it all goes shining, seething up.
fling off my hat it's the sooty cap of a mushroom
roll over and tilt my head back
                    over the edge of the dike.
yawn; shiny demons come out of space.
   this hay's soft, it's a first-rate bed.

clouds all picked to bits,
the blue becomes eyes in a huge net, an
underlying glimmering steel plate

           oriole without break —
      sunshining   crackling

• TRANSLATED BY GARY SNYDER •

REST

In the upper stratum of that resplendent space
bloom *kinpōge*
      (these are superior *buttercups*
        but they are not so much butter as sulfur and honey)
and below there are pearlworts and parsley.
Toy dragonflies made of tin are flying,
and the rain crackles
      (an oriole calls   calls

       besides there's even a silverberry)
I throw myself out in the grass,
and the clouds have both white spots and black spots,
everything glittering boiling.
I take my hat and throw it down and there a black mushroom top
     hat.
I draw myself up and my head goes to the other side of the mound.
I yawn,
and in the sky too a devil appears and shines.
      These dead grasses are soft,
        now this, an ultimate cushion.
The clouds have all been plucked,
and the blue has turned into a giant net.
That's the gleaming mineral plate.
      The oriole does his thing incessantly,
        and a skylark falls toward me, crackling

• 5 / 1 4 / 1 9 2 2 •

ANNELID DANCER (ANNELIDA TÄNZERIN)

      (Yes, it's water sol,
        it's opaque agar liquid)
Sun's a golden rose.
A red, tiny wormy worm,
draping itself with water and light,
is dancing a solitary dance
      (Yes, $8\ \gamma\ e\ 6\ \alpha$
        in particular, arabesque ornate letters)

the corpse of a winged insect
a dead yew leaf
pearly bubbles and
a torn rachis of moss
    (Red, tiny princess dear
    now above the bottom in the deep
    dances, yes she dances all alone
    only with a yellow fluff;
    no, but soon, it'll be soon,
    up she'll come in no time at all)
The red annelid dancer
with two pointed ears,
each metamere, phosphorescent, coral,
correctly adorned with a pearly button,
turns round and round, pirouetting
    (yes, *8 γ e 6 α*
    in particular, arabesque ornate letters)
With her back glistening
pirouette she does with all her might,
but her pearls, in truth, are all fake,
not even glass, but gassy beads
    (no, but even so,
    eight gamma E six alpha
    in particular, arabesque ornate letters)
With her back glistening
dance she does with all her might, or so I say.
But if, in truth, you leap about, tortured by bubbles clinging, all that
    isn't easy for you.
    Besides, the sun has set behind the clouds;
    I got pins and needles, sitting on a stone;

the black wood chip at the bottom of water looks, I say, like a
     caterpillar or a sea cucumber.
     Besides, first of all, I can't see your shape.
     Have you really melted away, I wonder.
Or, was all this an opaque blue dream
from the start, I wonder
     (No, she's there, she's there,
     princess dear, she's there
     8 γ e 6 α
     in particular, arabesque ornate letters)
Humph, water's opaque,
light's at a loss,
worm's eight gamma E six alpha
     in particular, arabesque ornate letters, you say,
     oh you make me ticklish
   (yes, I'm quite certain about that, sir
     eight gamma E six alpha
     in particular, arabesque ornate letters)

· 5/20/1922 ·

REPORT

The fire we made such a fuss about turned out to be a rainbow.
Already for one full hour it has maintained a dignified arch.

· 6/15/1922 ·

THE LANDSCAPE INSPECTOR

That forest
has too much verdigris piled into it.
I might overlook it if the trees were in fact like that,
and it may be partly due to the Purkyně effect,[3]
but how about
arranging to have the clouds send a few more olive-yellow rays?

Ah what a commendable spirit!
The frock coat shouldn't only be worn
in the stock exchange or parliament.
Rather, on a citrine evening like this,
in guiding a herd of Holsteins
among pale lances of rice,
it is most appropriate and effective.
What a commendable spirit!
Yes, his may be beancake-colored, tattered,
and a trifle warm,
but the serious manner in which he stands erect,
such a pious man in the landscape,
that's something I have never seen before.

• 6/25/1922 •

---

3. A perceptual discovery made by Bohemian physiologist J. E. Purkyně
(1787–1869).

HARATAI SWORD-DANCING TROUPE

dah-dah-dah-dah-dah-sko-dah-dah
Under tonight's crescent in its strange garb,
your hoods adorned with cocks' black tail feathers,
flashing single-blade swords,
you dancers of Haratai Village!
Throwing out your lusty swelling chests
toward the hardships of Alpine farming,
giving your ample shiny cheeks
to the highland's wind and light,
clothed in linden bark and ropes,
atmospheric warriors, you, our friends!
The vast air stretching blue, deep,
gather the melancholies of oak and beech,
hold up torches over serpentine mountain ground,
shake your cypress hair,
and in the sky with the smell of quince,
burn a new nebula!
dah-dah-sko-dah-dah
Letting humus and soil chisel your skin,
muscles and bones roughened in cold carbon acid,
you masters have accumulated your years piously,
agonizing over sunlight and wind every month.
Tonight's the festival of the Galaxy and woods.
Beat the drums ever harder
at heaven's end line of the semiplain,
make the thin moon's clouds reverberate
    Ho! Ho! Ho!

King Evil Path, of Tatta, of the past,
His dark dark cave five miles deep.
Going there is God of Black Night,
His head cut up and pickled.
The Andromeda shakes in the torches.
Blue masks a mere bluff,
Swords slashing, drown, drown!
Spider dance at the bottom of night wind,
Wearing stomachs, messy mess!
dah-dah-dah-dah-dah-sko-dah-dah
Make your swords meet ever harder,
invite from all around night's demons and gods,
even the tree sap trembles tonight, people!
Make your red robes flutter over the ground,
consecrate the hail-clouds and wind!
dah-dah-dah-dah
Night wind roars, cypresses in disarray,
and the moon rains down silver arrows.
Both winner and loser live as long as sparks
while the squeaks of swords last!
dah-dah-dah-dah-dah-sko-dah-dah
The swords are flashes of lightning, miscanthus rustles.
The rain of fireballs falling from the Constellation Leo
has vanished, traceless, on heaven's field.
Both winner and loser live a single life.
dah-dah-dah-dah-dah-sko-dah-dah

• 8/21/1922 •

A MOUNTAIN PATROLMAN

Oh
what a magnificent oak!
A green knight,
he's a green knight wet in the rain, standing erect.

In the blue dark of the chestnut trees,
that long thing drenched, washed by splashes and rain,
could it be a boat?
Or a sled?
It looks too Russian to me!

In the swamp grow willows and salad,
I mean, a salad of pretty reeds.

• 9 / 7 / 1 9 2 2 •

TRAVELER

You who go through rice paddies in the rain,
you who hurry toward leviathan woods,
you who walk into the gloom of clouds and mountains,
fasten up your raincoat, damn it.

• 9 / 7 / 1 9 2 2 •

BAMBOO & OAK

You say you suffer.
If you do suffer,
when it rains,
you'd better stay in the woods of bamboo & oak
    (*You* get your hair cut)
Yes, stay in the blue woods of bamboo & oak
    (*You* get your hair cut.
    Because you've got hair like that
    you think things like that)

• 9/7/1922 •

MASANIELLO

Above the waves of pampas grass in the castle[4]
is made-in-Italy space
where a flock of crows dance.
Several fragments of white mica clouds
    (moat, olive-velvet, cedars)
Are they silverberries? — glistening and swaying so.
Seven silver ears of pampas grass
    (below the castle, in the paulownia wood, swaying, swaying,
      the paulownia)

4. The poem title refers to Tommaso Aniello, known as Masaniello (1622–1647),
an Italian fisherman-rebel who was murdered five days after he was elected "leader
of the people." Kenji likely learned about this character from Daniel-François-
Esprit Auber's opera *La Muette de Portici,* better known as *Masaniello.*

Red flowers of knotweed move.
Sparrows   sparrows
they fly slowly to the cedars and enter the rice stalks.
Because that's by the bank and there's no air current
they can fly that slowly
        (because of the wind, the sorrow, I feel thick in the chest)
Is it all right to repeat his name
many times in the wind?
        (it's about time they came down the cliff
        with plows and ropes)
In the quiet sky where there are no more birds
again the crows enter sideways.
The roofs are oblong, their slopes shine white.
Two children run,
Japanese children flaunting their *hoari*.
This time parabolas of brown sparrows.
This side of the metallic mulberries
another child walks slowly.
Red, red are the ears of reeds.
        (it's Russia, it's Chekhov)
White poplars, sway oh sway
        (it's Russia, it's Russia)
The crows fly up again.
The flock of crows is zinc scrap in dilute sulfuric acid.
The sky above the castle is now white, Chinese.
Three crows slip down the cedar,
become four, turn and tumble.

• 10/10/1922 •

Before the day ends
you will be far away, my sister.
Outside, there's sleet and it's oddly bright.
    (Please get me some rain-snow)
From the clouds, reddish, all the gloomier for it,
the sleet comes down thick and clumsy
    (Please get me some rain-snow)
To get rain-snow for you
in these two chipped ceramic bowls
with blue water-shield designs
I flew out into this dark sleet
like a crooked bullet
    (Please get me some rain-snow)
From dark clouds the color of bismuth
the sleet sinks thick and clumsy.
Ah, Toshiko,
now so close to death
you asked me
for a bowl of clean snow
to brighten me for the rest of my life.
Thank you, my brave sister,
I too will go by the straight way
    (Please get me some rain-snow)
In your harsh, harsh fever, panting,
you asked me
   for a last bowl of snow that fell from the sky,

the world called the galaxy, the sun, the atmospheric strata . . .
. . . Between two slices of granite
sleet makes a solitary puddle.
I will stand on them, precariously,
and get for my gentle sister
her last food
from this lustrous pine branch
laden with transparent, cold drops
that maintain the pure-white two-phase system of snow and water.
Today you will part with
the indigo designs of these bowls we've seen
since the time we grew up together.
(Ora Orade Shitori egumo)[5]
Yes, today you will part with them.
Ah, in that closed sickroom,
behind the dark screen and mosquito net,
my brave sister,
you burn gently, pale.
No matter where I choose it
this snow is too white, everywhere.
From that terrifying, disturbed sky
this beautiful snow has come.

> (When I'm reborn
> I'll be born, the next time, so I won't suffer
> only for myself like this)

5. Perhaps because the utterance was in the heavy Tōhoku dialect, the original was written in roman characters. Kenji's note: "I, I'm going alone."

On these two bowls of snow you will eat
I pray from my heart:
may this turn into the food of Tushita Heaven[6]
and soon bring to you and all others
sacred nourishment.
That is my wish, and for that I will give all my happiness.

• 1 1 / 2 7 / 1 9 2 2 •

PINE NEEDLES

   some raindrops still clinging
— I brought you these pine boughs

— you look like you'd jump up
& put your hot cheek against this green,
fiercely thrust your cheek
into the blue pine needles
greedily
— you're going to startle the others —
did you want to go to the woods

                    that much?

burning with fever
tormented by sweat and pain

6. The region presided over by the Bodhisattva Maitreya. Maitreya, the Buddha-to-come, is the bodhisattva who will appear on earth to succor people 5,670 million years after the Sakyamuni, or Gautama Buddha, attains nirvana. The bodhisattva of love and compassion, Maitreya is regarded as the supreme being in Mahayana Buddhism. Kenji originally had here "May this become heavenly ice cream."

And me working happily in the sunlight
Thinking of you, walking slowly through the trees
    "Oh I'm all right now
    it's like you brought the
    center of the forest right here . . ."

Like a bird or a squirrel
you long for the woods.
how you must envy me,
my sister, who this very day must
    travel terribly far.
can you manage it alone?
    ask me to go with you
    crying — ask me —
your cheeks however
how beautiful they are.

I'll put these fresh pine boughs
on top of the mosquito net
they may drip a little
ah, a clean
smell like turpentine.

• TRANSLATED BY GARY SNYDER •

Here's the beautiful pine branch
I took the sleet from.
Oh, you almost leap to it,
pressing your hot cheeks to its green leaves.
The way you let the blue vegetable needles
sting your cheeks fiercely,
the way you look as if ready to devour them,
how it surprises us!
You have wanted so much to go to the woods.
While you burned with fever,
while you writhed in sweat and pain,
I was in the sunlight, working happily,
I was strolling idly in the forest, thinking of someone else.
((Ah good, I feel so refreshed,
as if I came through the woods))
Like a bird, like a squirrel,
you longed for the woods.
How you must have envied me!
Ah my sister, you will leave for a distant place before the day ends,
are you truly going alone?
Ask me to come with you.
Ask me, crying.
Your cheeks,
how beautiful they are!
Let me put a fresh pine branch
on the green curtain, too.
Soon drops will fall from it.

And look,
it's fresh.
Can you smell the fragrance of turpentine?

• 1 1 / 2 7 / 1 9 2 2 •

VOICELESS GRIEF

So closely observed by people
here you still must suffer.
When I deliberately leave the power of the great faith,
losing purity and a number of small virtues,
when I walk in the dark-blue asura,
you are going, alone,
the way set for you.
When I, your sole companion in the religion,
step out of the bright cold way of devotion, weary and sorrowful,
and drift in the dark field of poisonous grass and luminous fungi,
where are you going, alone?
    (Don't I look frightening?)
With such a resigned, painful smile
and trying not to overlook
the smallest expression on my face
you ask mother, bravely
    (No, you look fine,
     you look really fine today)
Yes, you really do.
Your hair is darker than ever,

your cheeks are like a child's, like apples.
May you be reborn in heaven
with such beautiful cheeks.
    ((But I smell bad, don't I?))
    ((No, not at all))
No, you really don't.
Rather, this place is full of the fragrance
of tiny white flowers of the summer field.
But I can't tell you this now
    (because I'm walking in the asura).
If my eyes look sad
it's because I'm looking at my two hearts.
Ah please do not turn your eyes away
so sorrowfully.

• 1 1 / 2 7 / 1 9 2 2 •

WHITE BIRDS

    ((All of them are thoroughbreds.
    Can anyone just go break them?))
    ((You've got to know the job terribly well))
Beneath old-fashioned Saddle Mountain
the tufts of field poppies stir.
Beneath the clear blue birches
several brown horses gather,
shine quite marvelously
        (The ultramarine of the sky in the Japanese scrolls
        and the turquoise of the horizon aren't rare,

but the corona of so large an imagination
is rare, in a landscape.)
Two large white birds fly
calling to each other sharply, sorrowfully
in the moist morning sunlight.
They are my sister,
my dead sister.
Because her brother has come, they call so sorrowfully.
    (This, on the face of it, is false
    but not wholly so.)
Calling so sorrowfully
they fly in the morning light.
    (It seems not to be morning sunlight
    but the afternoon, ripened, tired.)
But that's my *vague* silver illusion
after walking all night to get here.
    (For I saw the morning's gold liquid, crushed, molten,
    rise from the blue dream, the Kitakami Mountains.)
Why do those two birds
sound so sorrowful?
When I lost my power to save,
I lost my sister as well;
it's because of that sorrow
        (Last night in the moonlight in the oak wood,
        this morning in the swarms of lilies-of-the-valley,
        how many times I called her name,
        how many times a voice, I can't tell whose,
        responded from the end of the deserted field
        and jeered at me)
it's because of that sorrow

but in fact, their calls are sorrowful.
Now the birds, two of them, shine, a white arc,
descend in the marsh there, among blue reeds
and breaking off, rise again.

> (Before the new tomb of Prince Yamato Takeru[7]
> his wives lay prone and grieved.
> When plovers happened to fly up from it
> the wives thought they were his soul
> and bruising their feet among the reeds
> ran along the beach after them.)

Kiyohara stands there, smiling.

> (A real country child, shining, suntanned.
> His head, shaped like a bodhisattva, came from Gandhara.)

The water shines, a clear silver water.

> ((Come, there's water there.
> Let's rinse our mouths and go, refreshed.
> Because it's such a beautiful field.))

• 6/4/1923 •

OKHOTSK ELEGY

The sea is rusted by the morning's carbon acid.
Some parts show verdigris, some azurite.
There where the waves curl, the liquid is fearfully emerald.

---

7. A military hero in the *Kojiki* (The Records of Ancient Matters), a semimythological account of Japanese history compiled in 712 A.D.

The ears of the timothy, grown so short,
are one by one blown by the wind.
    (They are blue piano keys
    pressed one by one by the wind)
The timothy may be a short variety.
Among dewdrops, morning glories bloom,
the *glory* of the *morning glories*.
    Here comes the steppe cart I saw a moment ago.
    The head of the aged white draft horse droops.
    I know the man is all right
    because on that empty street corner
    when I asked him, Where's the busiest section of the shore?
    he said, It must be over there
    because I've never been there.
    Now he looks at me kindly from the corners of his eyes
        (His small lenses
        surely reflect the white clouds of Karafuto)[8]
They look more like peonies than morning glories,
those large blossoms of beach roses,
those scarlet morning blossoms of beach eggplant.
  Ah these sharp flower scents
  can, I insist, only be the elves' work
  bringing forth numerous indigo butterflies —
  here again, tiny golden lancelike ears,
  jade vases and blue screens.

8. The Russian name of this island in the Sea of Okhotsk is Sakhalin. Following the Russo-Japanese War (1904–1905), its southern half became Japanese territory. (The Soviet Union took back the southern half in 1945.)

Besides, since the clouds dazzle so,
this joyous violent dizziness.

    Hoof marks, two by two,
    are left on the wet quiet sand.
    Of course not only the horse has passed.
    The wide tracks of the cartwheels
    form a soft series.
Near a white thin line waves have left
three tiny mosquitoes stray
and are being lightly blown off.
Piteous white fragments of seashells,
blue stalks of daylilies half buried in the sand.
The waves come, rolling the sand in.

I think I'll fall upon the pebbles of white schist,
hold in my mouth a slice of seashell
polished clean by the waves
and sleep for a while.
Because, for now, from the sound of these waves,
the most fragrant wind
and the light of the clouds
I must recover the transparent energy that I gave
to the morning elves of Sakhalin
while I lay on the fine carpet
of blue huckleberries bearing ripe black fruit
among the large red blossoms of beach roses
and mysterious bluebells.
Besides, first of all, my imagination
has paled because of tiredness,

becoming a dazzling golden green.
From the sun's rays and the sky's layers of darkness
there even comes the strange wavering sound of a tin drum.

Desolate grass ears, the haze of light.
The verdigris extends serenely to the horizon
and from the seam of clouds, a variegated structure,
a slice of heaven's blue.
My chest retains the strong stab.
Those two kinds of blue
are both the properties that Toshiko had.
While I walk alone, tire myself out, and sleep
on a deserted coast of Karafuto,
Toshiko is at the end of that blue place,
I don't know what she's doing.
Beyond where the rough trunks and branches of white and silver
firs like in confusion, drifting, stranded,
the waves roll many times over.
Because they roll, the sand churns
and the salt water is muddy, desolate.
   (Eleven fifteen. Its palely gleaming dial.)
On this side of the clouds, birds move up and down.
Here a boat slipped out this morning.
The rut engraved in the sand by the keel
with the horizontal dent left by a large roller —
that's a crooked cross.
To write HELL with some small pieces of wood,
correct it to LOVE,
and erect a cross,

since that's a technique anyone uses,
when Toshiko arranged one of them
I gave her a cold smile.
>   (A slice of seashell buried in the sand
>   shows only its white rim.)
The fine sand that has finally dried
flows in this engraved cross,
now steadily, steadily flowing.
When the sea is this blue
I still think of Toshiko,
and the expressions of distant people say,
Why do you mourn for just one sister so much?
And again something inside me says:
>   *(Casual observer! Superficial traveler!)*
The sky shines so, it looks empty, dark,
three sharp-winged birds fly toward me.
They've begun to cry sorrowfully.
Have they brought any news?
There's pain in half of my head.
The roofs of Eihama[9] now distant, flare.
Just one bird blows a glass whistle,
drifting away in chalcedonous clouds.
The glitter of the town and the harbor.
The ibis-scarlet over the slope on its back
is a spread of fireweed flowers.
The fresh apple-green grassland
and a row of dark-green white firs.

---

9. A port town in Karafuto; now called Starodubskoe.

(Namo Saddharmapundarika Sutra)[10]
Five tiny sandpipers
when the sea rolls in
run away, tottering
(Namo Saddharmapundarika Sutra)
When the waves receded flatways,
over the mirror of sand
they run forward, tottering.

• 8 / 4 / 1 9 2 3 •

VOLCANO BAY: A NOCTURNE

Dextrin, the green gold of young peas,
where do they come from, and shine so?
 (The train squeaks; I sleep, tired.)
Toshiko opens her big eyes and
burned by a fierce rose-colored fire
 (That high July fever . . .)
was thinking of woods where birds live and the air is like water.
 (Was she thinking
 or is she thinking now?)
The train's squeaks, two squirrels.
 ((This year, those of you who aren't out to work —
 suppose you take turns going to the woods?))
says an obnoxious Arab chief,

10. Sanskrit for *Namu Myōhō Renge-kyō*.

a brass scimitar at his waist.
One day toward the end of July
Toshiko said, quite lost:

    ((I wouldn't mind dying.

    I must go to the woods.

    I wouldn't mind if I moved around, the fever got worse,

    and I was dead — if it was in those woods.))

Like a bird, like a squirrel,
she longed for the fresh woods so.

  (Squirrel squeaks are a waterwheel at dawn

  beneath a large chestnut tree.)

The year nineteen hundred and twenty-three
Toshiko opens her eyes gently
and in a transparent rosy fever
thinks about the blue woods.
The sound of a *fagotto* comes from ahead,
the *Funeral March* mysteriously begins again.

    (The train's squeaks, two sorrowful squirrels.)

  ((Do squirrels eat fish?))

    (On the second-class train window, frost designs.)

Daybreak isn't far off.
I clearly see the trees and the grass on the cliff.
The train's squeaks have grown husky.
A tiny, tiny white moth
crawls under the ceiling lamp.
(The train's squeaks, heaven's music.)
This reflection of daybreak light on Volcano Bay.
On the Muroran steam ferry,
two red lights.
The eastern horizon striped the color of muddy malachite.

Birches and boxwoods stand black.
Koma Peak, Mount Koma Peak,
rises, covered with dark metallic clouds.
In the coal-black cloud
Toshiko may be hidden.
Ah reason tries to persuade me again and again
but my loneliness remains uncured.
A different space that I do not feel
reflects a phenomenon, which was with me until now.
That's what makes me lonely.
     (We call that loneliness death.)
Even if in the different glittering space
Toshiko smiles gently,
my feelings are warped with sorrow
and I can't help thinking of her, hidden somewhere.

• 8/11/1923 •

COMMANDMENT ON NO GREED

To wear oiled paper, climb on a wet horse,
and go leisurely, in the cold landscape, by the dark forest,
over the slow, ring-shaped, eroded hill, among the red ears of
   miscanthus,
would be just fine,
and to spread a black polyhedral umbrella
and go to town and buy refined sugar
would be a very fresh project
     (Cheep cackle cheep cackle   the titmouse)

That the shrub of coarse grass called *Oryza sativa*[11]
has acquired a salad color
which even Turner would covet
is, according to the Most Reverend Jiun,[12]
a manifestation of the commandment on no greed[13]
      (Cheep cackle cheep cackle   the titmouse
      the then educated idler
      is now quite a reliable administrator)
The gleams of the gray fire line
on the dark mountain sputtering out loneliness
are also, according to the Most Reverend Jiun,
a manifestation of the commandment on no greed.

• 8/23/1923 •

LOVE IN RELIGIOUS MODE

When the coarse rice stalks have ripened in gentle oil-green
and, as for the west, it's filled with such a dark magnificent fog,
and grass ears, a field of them, are agitated by the wind,

---

11. Latin name for a species of rice.
12. Jiun Sonja (1718–1804), an erudite monk of the Shingon (True Word) school
of Buddhism.
13. *Fu-ton'yoku-kai* is one of the ten commandments stressed by Jiun, who said,
"If you live with the commandment on no greed and face colors, all the blue, yel-
low, red, and white are sufficient to nourish your eyes; all the pine winds and water
purling, like string and pipe music, are sufficient to please your ears."

your pitiful feeble brain
is disturbed blue, to the point of dizziness,
and your eyes, like Ōta Takeshi or the like,
are about to get gooey at the edges.
Your mind works so lopsidedly, pointedly,
yet why do you catch from this transparent beautiful atmosphere
what burns, is dark, is troublesome?
Why do you try to grasp firmly in the human
what you can get only in religion?
When the wind's roaring in the sky,
and the refugees from Tokyo, half suffering from meningitis,
still come every day,[14]
why do you deliberately take from the bright sky
the sorrow that shall never be cured?
This is no time for that.
No, I'm not saying it's good or bad,
I'm concerned that you're going too far,
I can't overlook it.
Come now, wipe your tears, collect yourself.
You must not love in so religious a mode.
That's where two spaces overlap,
absolutely no place
where we beginners can stay.

• 9/16/1923 •

14. A reference to the Great Kantō Earthquake, which struck the region on September 1, 1923, killing 100,000 people and leaving 1,000,000 more homeless.

Pale-blue sap oozes from the severed root.
I smell fresh humus
and work in the glittering air after the rain,
an immigrant puritan.
The clouds run, rocking dizzily.
Each of the pear leaves has precise veins.
On a branch with fruit-bearing blossoms a raindrop becomes a lens
accommodating the sky, the trees, the entire scene.
I hope the drop will not fall,
until I finish digging a circle here.
For, as soon as I remove this small acacia
I will politely bend down and touch my lips to it.
The way I look furtively in its direction,
in a collared shirt and tattered jacket,
shoulders squared as if I had a secret intent,
I may look like a terrible rascal,
but I think I'll be forgiven.
In the world of these phenomena
where everything is unreliable,
where you cannot count on anything,
the unreliable attributes
help form such a beautiful raindrop
and dye a warped spindle tree
like a gorgeous fabric
from rouge to the color of moonlight.
Now I have dug out the acacia,
I am content to lay down the hoe

and go under the tree, smiling generously
as if meeting my lover who's been waiting.
It is a form of desire.
Already it has become a water-blue past.

• 10/15/1923 •

SINGLE-TREE FIELD

As the pines suddenly brighten
and the field flashes open,
infinitely infinitely the dead grass burns in the sun,
electric poles gently relay the white insulators
on and on, to Bering City.
The clear ultramarine heaven,
a man's wishes cleansed —
larches again grow young and flare.
Ear's hallucination, transparent larks —
the blue rise and fall of Seven Showers[15]
rises and falls in the imagination as well,
and the willow trees in a cluster
are the willows on the bank of the Volga,
hushed in heaven's malachite bowl.
Yakushi's yellowish brown rises sternly, sharply,
the crater snow bears a distinct stripe in each wrinkle

15. A translation of *Nana-shigure,* an old volcanic mountain 1,040 meters (3,412 feet) high. So called because of its reputed changeable weather.

and Saddle Mountain's sensitive edge
raises nebula in the blue sky
  (Hey, oak,
   is it true your nickname's
   "tobacco tree of the mountain"?)
What a blessing
to be able to walk half a day
in such a bright vault and in grass!
I'd be glad to be crucified for it.
It's like having a glimpse of one's love
  (Hey, tobacco tree of the mountain,
   you better stop that odd dance,
   they might call you a futurist)
I am the forest and field's lover.
As I rustle ahead among the reeds,
a green epistle, modestly folded,
gets into my pocket, before I know it,
and as I walk in the dark parts of the woods,
crescent-shaped lip marks
cover my elbows and pants.

• 1 0 / 2 8 / 1 9 2 3 •

ICE FOG IN IIHATOV

Because we in fact had the first gallant ice fog in Iihatov
everyone welcomed it by taking out quinces and such.

• 1 1 / 2 3 / 1 9 2 3 •

WINTER & GALAXY STATION

Birds fly like dust in the sky,
heat haze and blue Greek letters
busily burn over the snow in the field.
From Japanese cypresses along the Great Passen Highway
frozen drops fall in shining abundance,
the distant signals of Galaxy Station
stagnate scarlet this morning.
While the river makes the ice flow away steadily,
the people, in rubber boots,
in fox and dog furs,
pretend interest in ceramic booths,
or size up the dangling octopi.
This is that noisy winter fair of Tsuchisawa.
(Alders and blinding cloud alcohol.
I wouldn't mind if a golden goal of parasites
was hanging coolly there)
Ah, the light railway of the Galaxy in winter
that Josef Pasternack[16] conducts
passes under many layers of feeble ice
(red insulators on utility poles and pine forest)
dangling medals of fake gold,
its brown eyes opened proudly,
under heaven's bowl that turns cold, blue,
it hurries over the sunny snowy tableland
(the ice ferns on the window glass
gradually turn into white steam)

16. A Polish-born American orchestral conductor (1881–1940).

The drops from Japanese cypresses on the Great Passen Highway
burn and fall everywhere.
Their blue branches that spring up,
rubies, topaz, and spectrums of things
are traded vigorously as in the fair.

• 12/10/1923 •

from SPRING & ASURA

(SECOND COLLECTION)

THE MOON ON THE WATER AND THE WOUND

To stand under the blue gleaming sea of wide air
and burn in so obviously pious a manner
a fragment of white *cigarette*
is to contribute to the negative of the moon's light and glitter,
to the cold moon on the water
    . . . but the wound on my right palm
        surrounded by the steel-blue isotherm
        throbs, throbs excitedly . . .
Hence, you should forgo the project of hunting for a piano
and play that medium-sized viola.
The pious, upright manner in which you stand
bathed in the ice crystals being woven in such light
is not appropriate for sallying forth for
a for-profit society, an ad with a prize
    . . . But from my palm
        blood drips pale blue . . .
    a shadow of a bird flitting across the moon,
    the electric poles, the music box,
    the water gas biting the mudstone,
    and a black line of buoys

... The blood on the palm
     freezing in the pocket
     perhaps emanates a faint phosphorescence ...
And yet, if after all
you cannot take my advice easily
your solemn ecclesiastical posture
will be no more than a factory of anxiety under the air sea —
in a verdigris overcoat bought on monthly installments,
with a moist ruby fire,
raising faint blue smoke,
it will be no more than a factory of anxiety.

• 2/20/1924 •

TRYING TO DRINK from the spring
you dropped your dog-skin glove in the mud,
but you shouldn't be so upset
splashing it about in the waves of pretty cress.
Look, the thatching villagers
smoking pipes, enjoying the sun
are snickering at you.

• 3/24/1924 •

SMALLPOX

About the time shadows suddenly lengthen
& dried leaves on the fence grow sharp
in the milky spring near here
the monstrous Scarlet School[17] becomes a fad.

• 3/30/1924 •

REST

The mid-sky is clear, warm,
except above the snow on the western ridge
where it stagnates, vague, white,
like a cloud in a crystal ball
        . . . chilled, sleepy, noon-rest . . .
There, dark cumuli
raise, like portraits, images of
the directionless *Libido* of
ancient troglodytes
while, on this side, flocks of larks
drift all over, singing
        . . . in the light, chilled, sleepy,
                the heroine of an old play pledges faith
                alone, lonely . . .

17. The old school of Lama, called the Scarlet School because the clergy wore red clothes.

From the eastern peridotite mountains
a cold wind blows down,
crosses canals one after another,
makes the thorny branches of acacia
and grasses past-prime sing,
draws a mysterious curve
with three stalks of mugwort
         (eccolo qua!)[18]
Through the wind innumerable dots of light float up and down,
and the group portraits of cumuli
now flow leisurely to the north.

• 4 / 4 / 1 9 2 4 •

THE WEATHER BUREAU

Shaman Mountain's right shoulder
has suddenly been covered with snow.
The highlands behind us too
are full of strange clouds,
extremely agitated.
    . . . The crop failure is at last upon us . . .
The cedars have all turned brown,
migrant birds have fallen, already many flocks of them.
    . . . Get me the carbon chart, will you? . .

18. Italian for "Here he is!"; this phrase appears in Mozart's *Don Giovanni.*

Now there are thunderclaps in the sixth zone.
The park is already
filled with townspeople.

• 4 / 6 / 1 9 2 4 •

THE CROW

Under the ultramarine heaven
through the reflections of the highland snow,
a transparent wind is blowing,
moving the rows of dull brown larches,
each differently.
A crow, in the ultraviolet rays that burn him,
perches on the core extending unusually long from one of them,
anxious to remember
a very old yellow dream.
The wind passes continuously,
the trees shake precariously,
the crow, like a rowboat
        . . . he's rocking it himself . . .
drifts in the waves of the winter heat haze.
And yet the many snow sculptures
lie too quiet.

• 4 / 6 / 1 9 2 4 •

THE SEA-ERODED TABLELAND

After the sun enters the final *sextant,*
the sky grows totally dull,
the tableland hazy, like the sea of boundless desire
    . . . The sea the color of illusion
        sadly yet nostalgically
           bites into the chest of the spring of continence . . .
There, the snow remains in a design of wave crests
and the larch woods and valleys
continue their hushed rise and fall
into the feeble smoke in the sky
    . . . It's a sea-eroded tableland
        an old marker stone of *kalpa* . . .
Climbing an unclear path
a slow band of highlanders
who might be taken for exhausted, self-tormenting Brahmans,
trailing a shadow of horses,
disappears in the smoke of cold air.

• 4/6/1924 •

MOUNTAIN FIRE

The blood-red fire
absentmindedly slides down the ridge
forms a monstrous crown
at the coal-black peak
lolls out a tongue of flame;

the agate needles shower
the willow's hair flusters
    . . . a dog barks frantically
        a lonely reflection on the marl cliff . . .
it changes into the shape of a corona or of a torn lung;
under this horrible enormous night-flower
            (Lord, Lord, your eyes are stained with blood)
drunk, cursing,
the villagers return.

▪ 4 / 6 / 1 9 2 4 ▪

FROM under a poplar
it abruptly splashed up out of the water
into moonlight.
Thought it was a fox
but it was that primitive pounder.
Beside it there is a tiny hut, too.
Must pound millet or something.
The water keeps pouring down,
spouting blue fire feebly,
the pounder is gradually coming down.
It drops water, and again springs up.
It's more a boat than a pounder,
more a spoon than a boat.
Feebly blue it's doing it again.
Somewhere a bell rings.
Both hill and pass keep quiet.

Grasses around me
utterly feel like birds in their sleepiness and softness.
In daytime soft buds of ferns
and *primula* must have been abloom.
To the left of my path, surrounded by chestnut trees,
in a bismuth-hued shadow,
a huge lock-shaped house stands black.
The bell must hang on the chest of a horse asleep
and tremble with its breathing.
Probably the horse, his legs folded,
is sleeping fragrantly on a bed of grass.
I'd like to sleep, too.
Somewhere a bird calls just like the bell.
It is, for example, a blue, blurry protective color.
Another calls over there in the shadow of the hill.
And then, beyond many a moonlit peak, in the distance,
rings a valley stream like a wind.

• 4/19/1924 •

RESERVOIR NOTE

At the corner I have just turned
two poplars stand
and with strings of male flowers hanging quietly from them
float against blue ice-clouds.
Withered grass is oddly dark,
a small stream the color of mercury

flows as in lacquer pictures,
and at each turn
a thicket blurs as in smoke.
By now, the schoolmaster,
far beyond the blue fields,
must have finished snip-snipping his hair
and gone to bed, legs outstretched.
Mr. Shirafuji the missionary,
emptied by his sermon,
must be sipping his bedtime tea.
No, all that could be last night:
maybe the schoolmaster is getting up with a dignified air
to write his next report,
and Shimaji Taitō's highest disciple, being so popular,
is walking intently
to catch the daybreak train.
Or perhaps
time's somewhere in between —
the shadow of my hat seems to suggest this last.
A Sharp pencil, the Moon-Mark,
a pale wind with the fragrance of beefsteak plant,
the moon in ripened cirri.
A silver hatchet, in the water or in my eyelids,
glints badly and shakes.
All day Takichi was cutting
a thicket of spindletrees
at one of the turns of this stream —
he must have dropped it on his way back.
Anyway the center of the sky

looks vacant, white, rough,
the wind is oddly sour. . . .
wind . . . and a twisted Judas tree,
the clouds over the sprawling fields
pale into mysterious stripes. . . .
I'll drop my pencil
the way a damson fruit
ripens and drops
and melt silently into the wind.
This whiff of fennel is it.

Wind . . . bones, the blue, somewhere a bell tinkles —
how long have I slept?
A blue star, solitary, beautifully transparent,
clouds, as if cast of wax,
dead leaves all look like birds' tail feathers,
and I tremble exactly like the leaves of the poplars.

• 4 / 1 9 / 1 9 2 4 •

SPRING

Since it's her duty,
spring comes, blue, uncomplaining.
If the way she hurries in, carrying on her back
a rainbow spanning the whole town,
if that's childlike,
it's pitiful the way she comes right beneath

the clouds curled in the shape of a heron.
    (Bonan Tagon, Shinjoro!)[19]
    (Bonan Tagon, Shinjoro!)
The cherry blossoms, in the sunlight,
somehow look like frogs' eggs.

              • 4 / 2 7 / 1 9 2 4 •

THE RAILROAD and the national highway
run parallel around here.
The electric poles cast bumpy shadows
in the fields already plowed.
The roadside trees, the pines,
lay their shadows neatly on the road.
In the small thatched stable
with a row of flowers planted on top,
a horse munches fodder.
A red-cheeked, barefoot child plays,
singing, pulling the three straw ropes
he attached to the stable door.
The willows flare against the blue sky.
The horses plowing the paddies busily go back and forth.
The smoke rises from grass fires,
and the mountains seem to flow, blue to the south.
The clouds shine quietly and break up.

19. Esperanto for "How are you, sir?"

The water tumbles softly on.
At the top of those glistening pines
a tall fire tower rises
and because the tip on one side is broken
a small russet-haired *goblin*
sits there and rests.
Resting, he looks around.
Far in the distance, where wind collapses,
gentle birds that feed on grass seeds
faintly rumble.
Just then, billowing silver smoke,
cleaving the air like a wedge,
an express train appears.
It runs very fast
but since each turning wheel is visible
the red-cheeked barefoot child
looks only at the train's feet,
holding the straw ropes behind him.
As the black train passes,
the giant man shouldering a three-pronged plow,
a longtime resident of the country,
stares after it with a silly grin.
Then he limps across the track to this side
and suddenly disappears, as if by magic.
The water again tumbles on
and the horse resumes munching.

• 5 / 6 / 1 9 2 4 •

In the south black shelves of cumulostratus have formed
and the two antiquated verdigris-colored peninsulas
mutually shed afternoon fatigue
    . . . the cross-meet point of two tides
      that often separates out sea fogs . . .
The waves are repeated specular reflections
of quietude, glittery dots, and angles of different species
or weave stripes of scallion-green and silver,
again, of the tin pest[20] and Prussian blue.
When the water, changing its seven-color costume,
is boasting to his companions
    . . . an Eastern-style wedding
      prone to rowdiness and transparent . . .
the ship lets its smoke flow south
and the water vein becomes a shockingly beautiful arsenic mirror.

Already the sunbeams to the north
contain the rise and fall of the Ezo[21] land
and again I view the black tail where rain clouds swirl.

• 5 / 1 9 / 1 9 2 4 •

20. The state of tin at a very low temperature when it becomes an ashen-white powder and looks "diseased."
21. An old name for Hokkaidō, the northernmost and second largest of the four main islands that make up Japan. Back when it was called Ezo, it was barely recognized as part of Japan. Its "development" began in the Meiji Era.

THE HORSE

After working one whole day among mugwort,
the horse, rotting like a potato,
feeling the juice of the bright sun pouring
on his rumpled head crusted with edible salt,
crunched, crunched, crunched on bear bamboo
at the edge of the field.
When the blue night came at last,
he returned to his stable
where, as if a high-voltage wire caught him,
suddenly he went wild, a mute struggle.
Next day he was cold.
They made an enormous hole
at the back of the pine woods,
bent his four legs,
and slowly put him down into it.
They sprinkled clods of earth
over his bent head.
They shed clods of tears.

· 5/22/1924 ·

COW

An ayrshire cow
playing, rubbing her horns in the grass,
            in the misty soil,

at her back the pulp factory fires
scorch the night clouds.
over low dunes
the sea booms
          a brass moon
like you could scoop up and swallow

so the cow feels pretty good
playing now
tapping the fence with her horns.

• TRANSLATED BY GARY SNYDER •

THE BULL

An Ayrshire bull is playing,
rubbing his horns in the grass and ground mist.
Behind him, the firelight of the pulp factory
scorches the midnight clouds,
and beyond the low dune
the ocean, pounding, pounding.
Yet, because the brass-colored moonlight
seems like you could scoop it up and drink it,
the bull feels good.
Now he's playing, butting the fence with his horns.

• 5/22/1924 •

TRANSITION OF A BIRD

A single bird is crossing scallion-green heaven.
I hear two calls of a cuckoo.
His body is terribly large,
and his course horizontal besides,
it's as though someone attached a spring to a model and flipped it.
I feel sorry for him that much.
The bird transits, his calls a while back, the axis of time,
make a graph of a blue arrowhead.
　　　. . . glisteningly folded mountain ranges,
　　　　aquamarine sky's green fringes . . .
His form no longer visible,
the bird is now crying
in the direction of my sister's cemetery
　　　. . . a yellow tram slides out of
　　　　the pines of the cemetery grove,
　　　　a glass pane trembles, shines,
　　　　another, side by side, shines . . .
The bird, before I know it, far behind me,
is turned into the grove of the brick factory, crying.
Or perhaps this is a different cuckoo.
The other fellow, his beak still shut,
may be looking up at the sky, as if wanting to drink water,
perched on a pine tree or something
behind the grave.

▪ 6/21/1924 ▪

MR. PAMIRS THE SCHOLAR TAKES A WALK

Because the atmospheric pressure has risen
the blue bulge on the horizon
which was spinning off clouds as disturbed as
solid forms of mercury yesterday
seems gradually to recover its level position.
And the quality of our land,
composed as it might be of lapis lazuli,
is not valued for its lack of elasticity.
The ground which, as one walks,
forms small disfigurements
may well be compared to gel.
That was a dream long harbored,
first in ancient India
and in time in countries in China's West.
This side of the volcano beyond of shining snow,
in a square field where some seeds have been sown,
what may be described as banners made of shavings
are erected correctly, twelve of them,
glowing in the evening sun the color of ancient gold,
flaunting variously in diverse winds.
No doubt they are some device with which to repel birds
and I have no special objection to them.
But the special way they are placed,
as if to enshrine that high mountain,
the long and the short occurring regularly,
correctly in two rows

suggests a legacy of some sky worship
or a custom traceable to some mountain sect.
Whatever it is, no one would overlook this scene
only as an accident produced
by a mere practical scheme.

I said, "The evening sun the color of ancient gold,"
and your eyes reproach me:
Why seize on despicable gold
to compare to this solemn evening sun?
By the designation, however,
I meant not the dark yellow matter
currently in traffic in the world
but, tracing far back into the past,
beyond the oceans of multitudinous emotions,
the kind that was slightly suggested
by the bodhisattva Nagarjuna[22] in his Great Discourse,
namely, its virtues still exalted,
its phases extremely active,
what should properly be termed quick gold,
that which makes your heart throb.

Yes, that in Kucha Empire's[23] evening sun
birds flowed through the air
just as smoothly as they do now

22. A Buddhist preacher and philosopher (ca. 100–200 A.D.).
23. An oasis city in the Uyghur Region south of the Tien Shan Range, where
Buddhism thrived. In the eleventh century Islam became dominant.

can be immediately pointed out
from the murals excavated there.
But whether the dragonflies called "tooth dye"
flew in the blue smoke over the marsh
is too faraway to be determined.

• 7/5/1924 •

IF I PASS through this forest
the trail returns to the waterwheel a while back.
The birds are crying glitteringly.
Sure to be flocks of migrant thrushes.
Throughout the night Galaxy's southern edge
glistens white, explodes,
fireflies flow, too many,
besides the wind incessantly shakes the trees,
so the birds, unable to calm down and sleep,
must be making so much racket.
Nonetheless
just because I've stepped in this grove,
they cry so fiercely,
so ever more fiercely,
just like a sudden shower,
how odd those fellows are!
Here it is a large grove of cypresses,
out of each of its pitch-black branches,
here and there snippets of the sky

variously tremble, breathe,
sending us catalogues of lights,
as it were, of every age
    . . . because the birds make so much racket
    I'm standing, dazed . . .
The trail flows away faintly white,
out of a dent of a stand of trees
muddied red Mars rises.
Just two birds came by in secrecy
and somewhat lucidly, lucidly, squeaked away.
Ah a wind blows and sends warmth, silver *Molekels,*
and the feel of every four-sided body.
Fireflies fly even more disturbed,
birds cry more busily than the rain,
and from the very end of the end of the grove
I hear the voice of my sister who died
    . . . though that may not be that
    it's the same with everyone
    so there's no need to think of it anew . . .
The heat of grass and the fragrance of cypress,
the birds begin another round of fierce racket.
Why do they make such a racket?
Even if people drawing water into paddies
tiptoe along the rim of the grove
or the stars in the southern sky often flow,
there's nothing perilous to you.
You can all sleep quietly.

• 7/5/1924 •

SPRING

The air melts,
heron-lilies have bloomed in the marsh.
The young girls, all of them,
let their sleek black hair slip down —
their new indigo petticoats
and aquamarine spring jackets.
On the steps of the bridge to the platform
the old bandmaster in red-striped pants
reads from his score,
as if to say, "It goes like this, boys."
The mountains flow faintly like smoke,
birds, flocks and flocks of them, pass
like the seeds of oats,
and a blue snake flies through the light of sky
on outstretched beautiful wings.
The train, Waltz Opus CZ,
has yet to show its white shape
on the horizon that quivers like a pudding.

· 8/22/1924 ·

SPRING: VARIATION

Various flowers' bowls and cups
as they open their august lids
and spurt blue and yellow pollen
some of it

falls, as it comes, into the marsh,
turns into whorls or stripes
and is quietly gliding, avoiding now here, now there,
the water stone-leek roots that poke out glaring green leaves.
Yet those girls standing on the platform,
one of them just never stops laughing,
all the others stroke her on the shoulders, on the back,
and do many things, but no matter, she doesn't stop laughing.

• 8/22/1924 •

WIND & CEDAR

On each one of the cedar's greenish-brown clusters
the dazzling white sky settles,
a digger wasp drones near my hot eyelids,
a wind blows, and a white building
         . . . . a white whistle a corkscrew. . . .
silver, pain, and a person who closes his mouth, lonely
         . . . . it looks like me, too
                  this platinum-haired beast's dazzling focus. . . .
half-melted, sparrows pass,
remembering, the wind blows
         . . . . I try but can't sleep. . . .
                  (come let your mother
                  into your sleep. . . .)
the dazzling afterimage of cedar needles
a dot, the white silver daystar
         . . . . eyelids are hot, the orange fire burns. . . .

                (at least get to be a devil in hell)
. . . . my lips bloom like a flower. . . .
once again dazzling white daystar

                :

                :

                (a blinker)
                (these got to be grapes)
. . . . faint red and gold. . . .
                (hey gimme work
                give me my work)

                :

                :

scarlet-coated railings
                (a peasant would find a different kind of work;
                you just, it's true, stand here
                making fun of people)
the copper-colored torso facing south
hair, kinky, gets mussed up in the wind
it looks like an Indian wrestler;
is that the tree god of this enormous cedar
or perhaps one of the winds?

                        • 9 / 6 / 1 9 2 4 •

CLOUD

You may say you came as fast as you could,
but it's like talking in a dream
like cheap wine

. . . . leaning against a wet midnight charred fence post . . .
Come, brother,
answer me
out of the coal-black cloud.

• 9 / 9 / 1 9 2 4 •

WHEN the wind comes
the man becomes a dynamo
          . . . white jacket flutters, flutters. . . .
trees all hang out blue lamps
clouds run across each other trailing tails
the mountain a single chameleon
indigo blue and sorrows
and various pigment particles
appear, disappear, there, busily

• 9 / 1 0 / 1 9 2 4 •

HARVESTING THE EARLESS MILLET

For a while, dazed, they face the westerly sun,
then busy again, bend their bodies
and start bundling the piled millet.
          Beyond them, children laugh.
          Women too, diligently,
          appear and disappear in a field the color of ancient gold

                    . . . all over the cliff a white fire
                        of pampas grass flowers . . .
Then, suddenly, they take a stance
and as if manipulating, as if pulling in, begin to sickle ahead
darkened, muddied, red millet stalks
                    ((kabe iiii i
                    nara iiiii i))
                        . . . the miscanthus ears are so bright
                            even the children get excited . . .
At the ends of the muddied, red anthocyanin millet
people work intently
                        . . . knotweed blossoms waver in the wind,
                            western clouds curl up, and wound . . .
        women too, diligently,
        swim in the dark sunset stream
                        . . . a flock of shrikes swoop into the miscanthus
                            a flock of shrikes swoop out of the miscanthus . . .
As if embracing, as if pulling in, they sickle ahead —
darkened, red millet stalks
                        . . . along the rim of the field
                            oily green row of hemp burns . . .
    ((dedeppoppo
    dedeppoppo))
                        . . . here, another group of children
                            brings a board into the street
                            and jump over it singing . . .
The children across the field have already vanished
far beyond wind and sunset.

                        • 9 / 2 4 / 1 9 2 4 •

WET in soggy cold rain,
relying on the faint phosphorescence of clouds,
I am walking tonight in love
with some bright windscape
of who knows when, some season of plums.
Now at midnight
I count one after another
each one of the houses vaguely asleep
surrounded with cedars and yews,
drift in the fragrance of rice stalks coming from I can't tell where,
hear absently in a distant sky
the voices of tired crickets and mutterings of water
and footsteps crossing puddles and mud
I can't tell whether mine or someone else's,
and while the larches make the wind lucid,
and the silver poplars disturb the clouds, swaying,
madly in love
with fragments of the bright words
innocently spoken
by the people with beautiful cheeks
who burn the red flowers of Oriental poppies
and pluck black plums,
through the rows of coal-black pines
endlessly I've come.
Ah must I make up for myself
what I am in love with?
I ask, shouting loudly
to the eastern sky,
and from a black forest near there

a mocking hollow voice
returns a fragment of the echo.
If you cast aside what you're in love with,
soon you'll be in love with love,
I mutter to myself, desolate.
I turn to see where I came.
An afterimage of the rows of pines
gleams palely in the sky.

• 1 0 / 5 / 1 9 2 4 •

NIGHT DEW and wind mingle desolately,
pine and willow go black,
the sky fills with dark petals of karma.
I have recorded the names of gods,
and shiver violently, cold.

• 1 0 / 5 / 1 9 2 4 •

GOOD DEVIL PRAYING FOR ABSOLUTION

Yeah I know that tomorrow, while it's still dark,
you've got to go to town with a horse cart full of charcoal,
but past midnight, in such moonlight,
you shouldn't be rustling about, hanging rice bundles up there.
Even far off in a field the color of thinned ink,
I heard the rustling.

You never know who might come with what complaints.
First of all, look,
look, over there,
the water in the paddies goes black like tooth dye,
the soybeans planted along the ridges start vigorous marches,
over the smoky thirteenth-day moonlight
a cross-shaped corona appears,
the sky takes on the look of a fish eye —
in short, things that aren't too good
are happening, one after another.
You'll be all right, floating up there
among the Amazon stones of the gleaming northern sky,
hanging bundles with a snotty air,
alone with greed in the windswept field,
but your precious wife on the ground
is tired, grown soft like sour milk
and totters back and forth, her mouth pursed,
trying to give you bundles of rice,
hooking one at a time at the end of a log.
After all, this was a bad year for everyone,
except that your rice took a good turn during the drought.
Now that's enough. Jump down, go home,
and until birds begin to fly across the sky,
have a good, solid sleep.

• 10/11/1924 •

EXCURSION PERMIT

Can you tell the random trails of wild horses
from the real paths?
You say, plantains, sainfoins,
but do you know what they really look like?

Can you pass by identical yellow hills
keeping track of them all?

Look at the firelines on your map.
How can you tell them from the ones made later?

Do you know what the underground stream is like
in peat strata?

Suppose you get lost anyway.
Can you rush home

through the oaks, withered scarlet,
and the big shrubs of deutzia and rose

following only the directions given by a compass?

Finally the sun goes down
and it may even sleet.
Do you still want to go?

I see, you do.

· 10/26/1924 ·

(I doze and the chill strikes)

(Gossamers are all blown crosswise)

(It's become a *fupicun*[24] mountain with snow atop it I say)

(Sir, did you have a sound and deep sleep last night?)

(Shall I say *Ja,* shall I say *Nein?*)

(Did you know of the midnight hail and thunder?)

(Wasn't aware of the thunder but heard sweet nothings)

(Aha! Shūshō, what, came to your room, didn't he,

with a methyl-mixed wine?)

(Besides that, he had put it in a sake bottle

warmed it lukewarm-like.

But I don't think it was methyl)

(No, he buys alcohol from a veterinarian and others

dozens of times, I hear.

Shūshō is quite a guy)

(He's gone off to a spring, has he?)

(He's asleep in the shadow of an oak)

(But he moved a lot in the morning.

Buried as many as ten marker stones, you know)

(Shūshō, you know what,

we told him every day,

She's a beauty with eyes yellow,

and that got to him, I think)

(I wonder about that)

(Well, the *gelbe Augen,*[25] too,

---

24. Or *fuhekishun,* the Japanese pronunciation of the Chinese word for "ax-cut stroke"; a style of Chinese painting that depicts a mountain as if it has been split with a hatchet.

25. German for "yellow eyes."

once it was decided to sell her,
but she's managed to remain like that)
(I know, horses are too cheap)
(Grandma was endlessly telling me,
roasting mushrooms, last night,
She may have grown up eating this and that
but that's a story too cruel for words)
(But isn't she marrying Shūshō?)
(To Shūshō? Don't know about that.
He deliberately put wild horses in the field
and lodged a complaint with the pasture owner,
Grandma was telling me that and other things)
(So they have no mind of marrying her, then)
(I'm tired of boiled cabbage!)
(Must be waiting for you in the Capital)
(That must be true of you.
How are you, it said, didn't it?)
(A bed of lilies-of-the-valley to relax on)
(And yet the bed has gotten old and yellow)
(Mountain peaks are already joyful)
(Canopy's scarlet, yellow & burning, why?)
(Java's usurping king munches on cucumber)
(Who'll inherit the throne from the breeze?)
(Adagio begins on a string)
(Oak shadow frosted leaves don't give up sweet nothings)
(Pappus lamp! Drummond light!)

• 1 0 / 2 6 / 1 9 2 4 •

FANTASY DURING A JOURNEY

After the desolate catch and the drought
I have come alone
along the coast
over countless hills
and through fields of miscanthus.
Now as I doze on the sand of a wild riverbed
in the weak sunlight,
my shoulders and back feel chilly,
somehow uneasy, maybe because
on the final dolomite hill
in haste
I left open the oak door
of the wood fence for pasturing.
Maybe because I did not close the white door
as it was,
the shining cold sky I saw there
and the chestnut tree with parasites come to mind.
Upstream, in the lattice of the layers of clouds
and cold rays of sun
an enormous bird unknown to me
faintly rumbles.

· 1/8/1925 ·

WIND & RESENTMENTS

Ponderous in fox fur,
you snatch from the wind such ridiculous resentments,
things that look like brass plates,
and throw them at me;
can't you see that I'm hurrying
along the pine road in the snow
and the ruddy cypresses lined up in the graveyard are watching,
I don't have enough time to respond to them one by one.
Ha!
in the cold sky over the town
a black smoke flows, flows.

• 2/14/1925 •

SHADOW FROM THE FUTURE

The blizzard drives hard
and this morning another catastrophic cave-in
        ... Why do they keep blowing
            the frozen whistle? ...
Out of the shadows and the horrible smoke
a deathly pale man appears, staggering —
the frightening shadow of myself
cast from a future of ice.

• 2/15/1925 •

Legs of the peak of snow and gabbro, in the tin light of the twenty-day moon, stagnant and red overfall pipes, the power station made of glass . . . and the pale waterfall at the spillway.[26] The dark snail-turbine makes an early rumble of spring thunder, shakes up the melancholy midnight sleepiness with the dynamo-coleoptera,[27] sends out spasms of thirty thousand volts toward the plain from six giant transformers; as he balmily monitors the fickle, emotional meters, before long the surrounding air grows warm like water and the giant fusulina[28] switchboard turns into a model of a traffic map, the toy train starts to run, and a gentle voice comes into his ears sleepier than the sea, Oh my lover's whole body's made of cool elegant ice, wearing valley icicles for shoes, thin ice on the abyss for mantle, and on her chest moves a potash-bulb twinkling. So you have three hearts after all, says the engineer sadly, lamenting, and the beauty puffs up her chest haughtily, You wouldn't be able to write a single scenario unless you had three or four hearts! The engineer suddenly turns furious, What on earth is this talk of a scenario? For your raggle-taggle learning and vainglorious reputation that's beyond silliness, the children in the fields around here can't even have small red pantaloons or socks, at the end of the year household heads come to the fish and medicine markets only to go to and fro sighing. So who on earth is the master who deserves such sacrifices, where on earth is the work that can stand up to such sacrifices? If art is something that rehashes an argu-

26. This poem is written in kabuki style, which is dominated by seven- and five-syllable patterns.

27. The order Coleoptera includes all species of beetles.

28. A large group of extinct single-celled organisms related to amoebas but with complex shells; well preserved, they are found as fossils in marine rocks.

ment or dodging an issue just for the sake of doing that, forever and ever the refuge for hoods and cowards, damn it, smash it up. I went too far, he thinks, and, sure, the Fraulein's whole body now the shape of Pisa's Leaning Tower, her gravity center seems to be coming out in front of her legs. Now, I'd like to know, why don't you jump back at me with a florid wit or a piercing taunt? Oh, the increase of a tilt angle is in proportion to the square of t! Things I said are all in a one-yen-a-copy book, hold steady, ma'am! But the lady, fainting blue and blue, collapses in jangling clatter. When, flustered, he opens his eyes, the workman's on the cold floor. He picks up his pliers. Outside the window it's all beneath the peak of snow and rough serpentines, from the factory of ferrosilicon a cloud of red parasol sparks is shooting up, and a line of clean, clear lamps is under a pale, twenty-day moon, in a bandit-gentleman-style wind.

• 4 / 2 / 1 9 2 5 •

SOME VIEWS CONCERNING THE PROPOSED SITE OF A NATIONAL PARK

Well how do you like this lava flow?
not very scenic, is it.
don't know how long ago it was spit out
on a sunny day like this you see the heat waves
just like a huge pan
and the snow up on the peak blue and simmering
say, have a sandwich.
why on earth don't you want to
develop this area?

it's a real good possibility —
mountains all around
crater lakes, hot springs, right there.
Saddle Mountain
well of course Saddle Mountain
and that big crater's probably
older than hell itself.
why sure! you could fix it up like Hell
with a real oriental charm to it, huh
a stockade of red spears
weird-shaped old dead trees put around
and plant flowers here and there,
well, flowers, I mean sort of things like uh
jimsonweed and viper grass
black wolfsbane and such
anyhow, make it gruesome, huh.
tourists will flock from all over.
we could get some mean looking guys
shave their heads
and make gates out of rock here and there
and drag the folks that come, around barefoot
              — you know —
by the "cuckoo singing on the path after death"
and the "ford of the river of the three ways"
"the gate to the new womb" at Yama's office
then, having expiated all their sins
we can sell them certificates for Heaven.
afterwards — at those three wooded hills
we could put on symphonies, huh
first movement: allegro con brio, like springing forth

second movement: sort of "andante"
third movement: like a lament
fourth movement: feeling of death
you know how it goes — at first kind of sorrowful
then bit by bit getting joyous.
at the end, on this side of the hill
hide two field-cannons
shoot them off — live shells — with a bang, by electricity.
just when they're feeling A-1
they'll *really* think they're on the
                   River of the Three Ways, huh
us we'll have had lots of practice
we won't be scared at all
I wouldn't be a bit flustered
say, have one of those sandwiches
that hill over there — really drizzling, eh?
like a picture in blue on a porcelain
that fellow will make a good backdrop, huh.

• TRANSLATED BY GARY SNYDER •

AN OPINION CONCERNING A PROPOSED
NATIONAL PARK SITE

What do you make of this lava flow?
It's bleak, wouldn't you say?
I don't know when it last flowed out
but when the sun shines like this the air whirls and boils,
it looks like a large kettle.

Even the snow at the top looks blue, cooked.
Well, have some bread.
Why don't you all
start a campaign
to propose this as a national park?
Possibilities?
There are plenty.
Of course I mean the whole mountain.
The crater lake back there, the hot springs, of course.
Saddle Mountain, too, needless to say.
Let me tell you something about Saddle Mountain.
You might call it Ur-Iwate —
it was the rim of a large crater
long before the Great Hell.
And yes, here in particular, set up a Hell.
Make it charming the Oriental fashion.
A spear-shaped red fence.
Touch it up with dead trees starkly.
Plant flowers here and there.
I said flowers, but they've got to be things like
Thorn apple, adder grass
and wolfsbane,
you know, devilish things.
Then, when all's done,
and villains and scoundrels
gather from all over the world,
shave their heads.
Set up gates here and there with stones,
cuckoos over the Mountain Path to Death,
cross the Three-Way River on foot,

Six Realms' crossroads,
from Yama's Courthouse to the Womb-Trip — [29]
through these, pull them around, barefoot.
Then, as a token of the remission of sins,
get them to buy false indulgences to Heaven.
In the end, at Mt. Three Forests
you play a symphony:
first movement, *allegro con brio,* as if leaping,
second movement, *andante,* as if groaning a bit,
third movement, as if aggrieved,
fourth movement, the feeling of death.
As happens often, first very sad,
then work up to ecstasy.
As a finale, blast off real shots electrically
from two field cannons
hidden this side of the mountain.
The moment they think, *Bingo!*
they're right there in the Three-Way River, you see.
But they'll first get preparatory exercises here
so no one will be confused the least bit, nor will I.

29. After death one is destined to spend the first seven days climbing up and down a steep path, where the cuckoo, the messenger of death, calls. Then one crosses a river in one of three ways, depending on the sins one committed while alive, before reaching the world of the dead, where Yama is the presiding deity. This notion seems to derive from the Ten King Sutra, the "fake sutra," concocted toward the end of the Tang Dynasty by combining Buddhist elements with Taoism. When it came to Japan it incorporated Shinto elements. *Sanzu no kawa,* the Three-Way River, is often compared with the River Styx. The practice of *tainai-kuguri,* "ducking through the womb," may be largely of Shinto origins, with some Buddhist elements. One may cleanse the body and spirit by passing through a narrow passage like a cave or hole.

Now, have some bread.
The mountain there, Seven Showers,
an indigo picture painted on earthenware —
that, you see, will be the backdrop.

• 5/11/1925 •

DROUGHT & ZAZEN

While the muddy, froth-flecked water of the seedling beds
reflects the shadow of a tin-colored heron
moving vaguely from one side to the other
the frogs' all-night chorus
drones into a sleepy dreary morning.
Today too, there will be no rain.
Here and there on the ridges
near the paddies where they just planted rice
they squat, motionless
each weighing the same koan
repeated for the last two days and nights. . . .
In the blue dark beneath the chestnut,
over the water-trickling drain,
with the stele, the Three Dewa Mountains, at my back,
and in direct view of the scene,
I calculate again and again
the number of days before the delayed rice takes root,
the number of days before bifurcation, and the time when the ears
    will come out.

The stone is cold,
the thin cloud-strips grow lucid,
and to the west the row of rock-bells darkens.

• 6/12/1925 •

THE IWATE LIGHT RAILWAY: JULY (JAZZ)

Skirting the jagged gabbro mountain,
along the coast of the seventh Kitakami tributary
that makes cold colloid waves flow,
impatiently trembling, often terribly jumping up,
rushing down headfirst toward the plain to the west,
it's the Iwate Light Railway's
last train today.
Whether you make a summery *love scene,*
eyes looking particularly bedazzled
or think depressingly about iridosmine deposits,
sliding by tree shadows,
making finest particles of snow near Taneyama glitter,
the train roars along.
Through patches of evening primroses
and a blue fire of irises,
dancing crazily,
be it a scarlet split plateau gravel at the end of the Tertiary Period
or a path by a cliff of diallagite,
whether there's a rock or two fallen on the track,
whether a cumulus gets burnt or collapses,

this is the last train of the entire line.
It doesn't care whether there's a *signal* or a *tablet,*
you can't jump on, it doesn't let you on if
you can't jump off,
it'll take you all the way
to Great Resort City near the North Pole and let you off,
or it'll guide you to a mysterious job
near the Galaxy power plant or the mine of crinkled lead clouds to
   the west,
messily mixing up winds in the valley and white fireworks.
Whether you *kiss* or pull a fraud,
the window glass quakes, trembles, clutter-clutter, shudder-shudder.
Be it a mountain field two hundred, five hundred yards long
or a collapsing sweetfish weir,
everything flies backward one after another,
as it rushes down to the plain headstrong.
      Our westbound train
      does not necessarily run on track;
      the vibration therefore can be unusual.
      But because it can also resolve blood stasis
      . . . Prrrrr Pirr! . . .
      and soften up your cardiopathy,
      this can be effective on excitable and tense people.
I see, after all, I should have done the prospecting for iridosmine and
   platinum mines
in sandy ores rather than in disseminated deposits.
Or shall I try, at least once, Ahara Pass or Esashi Sakai?
Nope, those are beyond my perseverance — whether you think that

or, *Love is easy, my wildflower,*[30]
I shan't change all my life,
so a knight's pledge may resound with a strong *base,*
this and that and everything else are just land blocks, summer
    bubble.
Dancing and jumping up like a dolphin,
already the tunnel where the cumulus was burnt behind it,
pine groves exhaling verdigris
folded away one after another behind it,
rushing down to the plain still more single-mindedly,
operated by our dear engineer, Mr. Fusa,
it's the Iwate Light Railway's
last down-train.

· 7/19/1925 ·

RESIDENCE

In the crescent-shaped village south of it
with a blue spring
and many abandoned houses
they say they don't want to accept

30. The title and first line of the lyrics Kobayashi Aiyū wrote for Franz von Suppé's light opera *Boccaccio,* first staged in Japan at Teikoku Theatre and then at some houses in Asakusa in 1919. It remained enormously popular until about the time the Great Kantō Earthquake struck, in 1923.

a teacher turned seed collector
    .... wind's light
        and grass seeds' rain. . . .
Even daytime, barefoot and drinking
those blear-eyed old men

• 9 / 1 / 1 9 2 5 •

A VALEDICTION

How the triplet of your bassoon sounded
you may not know. Its joy
innocent and full of yearning
made me tremble like a blade of grass.
When you clearly know and are able to command
the characteristics of those sounds
and their numerous arrangements,
you will do heaven's work, painful and resplendent.
While the noted musicians of the West
took to strings and keys in childhood
and in the end became famous,
you took to the products of this country,
hide drums and bamboo pipes.
Now, among the thousands in the towns and villages
who are your age,
perhaps five have your gift and power.
But every one of them, I say

every single one of them will lose
in five years most of what they have.
Either their lives will wear it down
or they will lose it themselves.
Talent, power, ability don't all
stay with a person.
(Even people don't stay together)
I didn't tell you
but in April I won't be in school.
Perhaps you'll have to walk a dark, hard way.
But then, if your power dulls
and your beautiful sound loses its rightness and brilliance
to the point that you can't recover it,
I will refuse to see you.
What I hate most
is the majority that rests in comfort
upon its mediocre accomplishments.
When you listen to me carefully —
when the time comes that a gentle girl fills your heart,
an image made of innumerable shadows and lights will appear
    to you.
You must make music out of it.
While others live in town or waste their time,
you alone will reap the grass in Stone Field.
With that loneliness you must make music.
You must take all the insults and poverty, and sing.
If you don't have an instrument

—remember you are my disciple
play, as best you can,
the organ made of light
that fills the whole sky.

• 1 0 / 2 5 / 1 9 2 5 •

THE NATIONAL HIGHWAY

What's making that scratchy noise behind the wind?
I guess it's someone breaking firewood from the roadside pine.
It's stopped —
they must be listening to me.
As I pass by,
they stand around, looking innocent.
The younger boy, just a kid with round cheeks,
eyes me vaguely.
Suddenly his big brother poises a pole, looking up,
as if aiming at a bird.
The pole has a small sickle at its end.
The sky is cold,
the white mountains mushroom,
and as for the large pine,
oh well, the contractors will cut it down anyway
to add to the cost of the public hall in Morioka.

• 1 / 1 4 / 1 9 2 6 •

SPRING

When the sun shines, birds sing,
the oak woods here and there
grow hazy,
I'll have dirty palms
that make a gritty noise.

· 5/2/1926 ·

SOMEHOW I walk up
to roadside cut branches and touch them,
and turn at a whitish wind:
in many spots dark groves for windbreaks
and rice stalks flowering and fallen all over the place
glowing in the rain under black clouds.
Over there are dozens of gloomy hamlets
where a while back I avoided sharp sidelong glances
or jeering words; well then
what is it that makes my heart
pound in such a foolish way?

The trail of hope I held this morning on this path faded,
now the eastern sky that slightly opens up white
is just what it is; well then
why is it that my heart pounds
even harder
as if there were excellent grounds for it?
At the end of the grass field a horse cart is small,
the man scantily pointed, blurred.

· 6/20/1926 ·

THE SNAKE DANCE

With this budding willow branch
let me tap him on the head.
Tapped, he slithers around,
so sensuous and clumsy.
He's no rattlesnake
but rustles his tail anyhow.
Item: though not of the tail-resounding species,
a snake may still make a noise.
Blue,
blue,
his pattern too is blue, magnificent,
a magnificent *rhythm*.
Yes, that's the *pose*.
The theme of this one must be
"White Lightning Attack."

Finally he opens his pinkish mouth,
an act comparable to the pose
the actor strikes, a little nervous.
Let me poke him a little more.
I have to handle manure today
so I'm fooling around with a snake.
But, snake,
teasing you
is like eating a sour tomato.
Are you getting out?
Well, then, so will I.

• 6/20/1926 •

FIELD

A shower pours,
kicks up the earth, the dust;
     ah, bathed in the rising steam
     I'm alone, resent the work
          . . . dead leaves of fern
           a wild rose root
           around the tower that fell to pieces
           ants now run busily . . .
Cedars put on the streams of shower,
again cast up faint, white splashes.

• 7/15/1926 •

THE CORN BAKING in the blue smoke,
Ponderosa piled on my plate,
I look at the *chrysocolla* of upper cedar branches;
it ought to be a joyful, sumptuous breakfast
but I'm restless perhaps because
I can't stop thinking of tilling the barren land
by the river today as well
     . . . enamel cloudbird's voice . . .
I force myself
to tear the fluffy scarlet hair off another ear of corn
and peel its aquamarine husk,
and that hot, painful work
feels like something faint a hundred years old.

• 8/27/1927 •

BANQUET

Crunching on sour cucumber
everybody's drinking sake
   . . . the earth bridge finished in the cloudy morning
     now the bluish smoke from kindling
     starts to crawl all over the rice stalks
     while the rain splashes, splashes
     on cedar and oak along the bank edge. . . .
Everybody's drinking sake
collected from landowners and those who were out for statutory work

. . . despite myself
    I absently say varieties of rice.
    Is this the Northern Route of Tien Shan . . .
The swollen-faced, feeble-looking boy
who a while back
was made to carry red gravel ten times
sits on the wooden floor behind everybody
eating wheat
    (Plant milk-vetch you get rice you say
    but all you get is straw's no use)
The child stops eating wheat
and casts a stealthy glance at me

• 9/3/1926 •

DISTANT LABOR

Beyond the pampas-grass flowers
    and the dark grove
a new sort of wind is blowing
— through dazzling wrinkly cloud fretwork
        and spring sun
with a shiver of strange odors.

And from the hill behind the empty creek
and the barely rising black smoke
of the tile works
a big cheerful racket.

— listening in the farmers fields
it seems pleasant enough work all right
but every night Chuichi
comes home from there exhausted
                    and bad-tempered.

• TRANSLATED BY GARY SNYDER •

DISTANT WORK

Beyond the miscanthus flowers and dark woods
some different specimen of wind is ringing.
In the lattice of glistering kinky clouds and blue light
the wind, with a mysterious fragrance, is trembling.
Reflecting the sky the river's empty
and a brick factory raises a bit of smoke.
From the table behind it
the echo comes clear, again.
Listening to it here, in the vegetable patch,
it sounds like a pleasant, bright sort of work.
But at night Chūichi returns from there,
tired, furious.

• 9/10/1926 •

CABBAGE PATCH

You stick a straw into the root
of each stolen cabbage
and call that Japanism,[31] do you.

Rows of aquamarine columns
with entasis have
their Suiko-era foundations left[32] —
when a straw is erected on each of them,
whenever a thief passes by,
it wavers in early winter wind, shining in the sun,
and surely derides him.
But you call that a victory
of Japanese thought, Iyasaka-ism,[33] do you.

• 10/13/1926 •

31. In Japanese, *Nihon-shugi,* a movement touched off by a call, in 1888, for the adoption of Japanese traditions in politics, economics, culture, and every other arena. Japan was in the midst of rapid Westernization at the time.

32. Suiko (554–628) was Japan's first ruling empress. During her reign (592–628), Japanese culture, which was under great foreign influences, thrived. The tradition of building temple columns with entasis, for example, is thought to have reached Japan all the way from the Middle East.

33. Iyasaka-ism, a part of Japanism, refers to shouting *"Iyasaka!"* (Ever More Prosperity [to Your Majesty]!) instead of *"Banzai"* (Long Live the Emperor), perhaps because the latter was originally Chinese.

HOSPITAL

On the way the air was cold bright water.
In fever, we become lively as fish
and feel very fresh, don't we?
The last cactus was burning, it was dazzling.
The streets and the bridge shone distinctly
and the people I met were all dressed
like the hummingbirds that immigrated to Iceland.
I imagine such precise outlines are not found
even among crystal forms under *mikroskopisch Analyse*.

• 11/4/1926 •

FLOWERS & BIRDS: NOVEMBER

(Tōhoku Chrysanthemum Contest: in Morioka)

(I'm saying, take the colors, for instance.
An old wood-block book says something like
"Only the Right Colors, such as white & yellow, are valued,"
that becomes the golden rule,
they never get out of those categories.
Now this just won't do.
When everything else is changing
and women & children think first about individuality
even in buying a single string,
the chrysanthemums can't follow
that "White is for paper, yellow for straw"

kind of nonsense.
I'm saying, they should start giving prizes
to sophisticated off-shades
to stimulate the whole thing)
(You are quite right, sir)

• NOVEMBER 1926 •

CROWS IN A HUNDRED POSTURES

Along the snowy paddy ridge
crows shuffle on in a row

Body bent on the snowy paddy
a crow utters two calls

Head down on the snowy paddy
a crow eats snow pecking at it

Head up on the snowy paddy
a crow takes a look around

On the snow in the snowy paddy
a crow waddles, waddles

Reaching the end of the snowy paddy
a crow eats snow pecking at it

At a height of the paddy snow
a crow has her mouth agape

His beak in the paddy snow
a crow keeps himself still

Onto a dry ridge of the snowy paddy
a crow gives himself a jump

With a rudder over the snowy paddy
a crow makes a slow flight

Over the snowy ridge in succession
crows fly up toward the west

Left behind in the snowy paddy
a crow keeps his legs apart

The crows flying toward the west
are now just like sesame seeds

THE BUCKETS climb
and out of the leaden shadow of the gauche rectangle
brimming with waves now warm, peaceful
I come into the sunlight
and there — a petal —
          — a sensuous shell —
     — a tuft of the *helichrysum* —
A moth lies flat
From the smooth powerful surface tension
struggling to separate its four wings
the moth writhes, writhes
     — here they go again, many tiny bubbles —

I must reinaugurate unto the ocean of warm shining air
this early lunger into the spring
the forerunner of lepidopterous swarms
A tiny cloud of spray
Scale-powder, bubbles, iridescence
The spring moth beats the water
and by itself flies

           up

      up

  up
and now sails through the brown tresses of cedars
and the indeterminate forms of clouds

▪ 3/23/1927 ▪

CULTIVATION

When we finally got rid of
the wild rosebushes,
the sun was blazing,
the sky was vacant, dark.
Taichi, Chūsaku, and I
wanted to fall just the way we were into bamboo grass
and sleep zz zz zz zz.
The river was carrying nine tons of needles a second
and a number of herons flew east.

▪ 3/27/1927 ▪

SAPPORO CITY

The gray light avalanched in the distance.
Over the sand of the distorted square
I turned my sorrows into blue myths
and scattered them
but the birds would not touch them.

• 3/28/1927 •

AMBIGUOUS ARGUMENT ABOUT
A SPRING CLOUD

If that black cloud
startled you,
I'd say it's mass psychology.
A hundred miles along the river
tens of thousands of people like us
who plow the wheat fields
and shear mulberry trees
now turn their passion to fight the winter
to vaguely sad, nostalgic thoughts,
to faint hopes,
and, not knowing where to look,
cast their eyes to the cloud.
And that's not all.
That muddy, dark mass,
a catenary of warmed water,

that, I must tell you, is love itself —
the interchange of carbon gas,
mendacious spring sensation,
that, I must tell you, is love itself.

• 4/5/1927 •

PIG

A Yorkshire pig, a large one,
cornered by the middle daughter,
has turned into fierce golden hair
and, tilting worse than a top,
is running away toward the westerly sun,
along the hem of the black forest,
running blind.
A stick over her head, hair glistening,
the daughter of a tribal chief of Japanese Province.
Beyond a withering zelkova tree,
rocking, the copper sun.

The village chief in blue hemp plops out of the forest,
and munching on something,
body stuck out this side of the forest,
shades his eyes with his hand and looks up at the sky.

• 4/7/1927 •

MALICE

With the black clouds swept together during the night
scorched by the sun climbing the mountains,
a ferocious, dark morning has come.
For the design of the playground today
I'll use the gray and red
that are on the hem of that devilish cloud.
I'll use something like
antirrhinum shaped like a fish with an open mouth
or base *hardy phlox.*
In this prefecture where there's nothing to eat
I'll pour a million
and will eventually come up with a devil's den.
This is a color scheme fit for it.

· 4/8/1927 ·

NOW burnt-out eyes ache,
the view they cover becomes twilled and sour.

Friends,
isn't the world
wholly made of blue fat?

· 4/11/1927 ·

IN Dōshin-chō toward daybreak
a line of soft electric lamps,
out of the springlike scallion-hued haze
a vague, blurred eastern sky;
on this side of it, sepiolite,
Teikichi, leading a horse,
falls alongside me,
and as we walk toward town
again gives me a sidelong glance.
If the reason is the green snow cabbage
in my rear cart,
that's a kind of envious look,
but it'll dry up light and fade tomorrow.
If the cause is the ears of six hyacinths
I cut off and am bringing along,
that's also halfway an envious look,
but I can take care of that by not growing them.
If he, unable to fathom
what kind of monstrous thought I have in me,
is looking at me like that,
I'd say he's fearful of me.
If I say things more clearly
and act more normally for a while,
that too will fade in no time.
We went to school,
we grew up in town,
we once drew monthly salaries —
if it's a suspicion
or a vague resentment of all that,
I won't be able to get rid of it with ease.

Ahead, where the downslope begins,
three dogs are playing with one another.
A child plops out.
When I get there
the child shouts, Give 'em to me! Give 'em to me!
pointing to my hyacinth flowers —
a routine every morning
Look at the new Berlin blue, sir.
The proprietor of the booth,
after painting it stroke by stroke, abandoned it,
and now under the small stone roof
where the walnut tree spreads its branches,
is about to fall asleep, isn't he?

• 4/21/1927 •

THE UNRULY HORSE

Kanesuke's manure horse
suddenly rears.
Eyes scarlet,
it turns into a dragon,
tries to rake in the blue velvet,
the spring sky.
A manure bundle tumbles down.
Cloud beacons rise all around.
On the bank wall where daylilies bud,
magnolia flowers and the blue of the mist.
Kanesuke grips the bridle with both hands,

pushes the horse half against the bank.
The horse struggles a few more times,
finally drops its enormous head,
gives up the thought of becoming a dragon.
You have no right to keep watching
someone's horse go wild.
Your plow glinted
and that frightened him,
Kanesuke says quietly, resentful,
bending over the spilled manure.
For the last two days
he's been in the dark stable,
tying up hot, sickening manure into hundreds of bundles,
and he's mad at the world.

• 4/25/1927 •

THE POLITICIANS

Running around here & there
stirring up trouble and bothering people
a bunch of lushes —
                fern leaves and cloud:
the world was so chilly and dark —

Before long that sort
will up and rot all by themselves
and be washed away by the rain
and afterward, only green fern.

And when humanity is laid out like coal
somewhere some earnest geologist
will note them in his notebook.

• TRANSLATED BY GARY SNYDER •

POLITICIANS

All of them want to make a racket
here and there and everywhere
so that they can have a drink or two.
        leaves of fern and clouds
        the world is that cold and dark
But soon
such bastards
rot of themselves,
get washed away in the rain of themselves.
What remains will be hushed blue fern.
And that this was the Carboniferous Period of mankind
a transparent geologist somewhere
will record.

• 5/3/1927 •

DEVIL'S WORDS: 4

If you suffer so much from peace
I'll send into your home
the family surviving that execution.

· 5/13/1927 ·

WE LIVED together
just one year.
She was gentle and pale,
and her eyes seemed
always to dream
of something I didn't understand.
One summer morning, the year we were married,
at the bridge on the outskirts of town
I saw a village girl bring flowers.
They were so beautiful
I bought twenty sen worth and brought them home.
My wife put them in an empty goldfish bowl
and put it on a shelf in the store.
When I returned that evening
she looked at me
and smiled a mysterious smile.
There on the dinner table I saw various fruit,
even white Western plates, among other things.
I asked what happened.

During the day the flowers had sold
for two yen exactly, she said.
        . . . That blue night's
            wind, its stars,
                the bamboo blind, the candles sending off souls . . .
The following winter,
my wife, without suffering,
as if withering, as if dropping away,
was ill a day, and died.

• 6 / 1 / 1 9 2 7 •

THE PREFECTURAL ENGINEER'S STATEMENT REGARDING CLOUDS

Although mythological or personified description
is something I would be ashamed to attempt,
let me for a moment assume the position of the ancient poet
and state the following to the black, obscene nimbus:
I, a humble official, hoping to wash both mind and body
in the vast air glimmering above this summit,
and in the cold wind passing here with a fragrance of roses,
and in the terrifying blue etching of mountains and valleys,
have managed from today's business schedule
a few moments
and stand here, knowing their full value.
But, first of all, black nimbus,
against my wish

you bring to mind an abnormal anxiety
and make me feel as if I were, in the words of the *Kojiki,*
"treading on air."
Let me explain, since you ask the reason:
For two-thirds of this past May,
obscene family of nimbus,
you covered the river and the valley to the west and did not move.
As a result, sunlight fell below the normal level
and all the rice seedlings grew excessively
or acquired red splotches.
Under the circumstances, as outlined,
I could not regard without grave concern
the season's rice growth in this prefecture,
I looked up at the skies and uttered anguished cries
more than several times a day.
Last night, however,
the veteran weather bureau chief
forecast it would be absolutely sunny,
and this morning, the sky blue, the air fresh,
I enjoyed letting my cigar smoke flow out the train window,
the fifty miles among valleys and twenty-five miles through plains,
happy to be on schedule. But now, past noon,
what deceit, what breach of trust!
As I scan the vast expanse from this summit,
I am gnawed by anger:
First, that you, from here to the east,
disguised in the color of the nightingale,
cover the long stretches of landmass
to the limit of visibility

to rape the ocean;
second, that you rush northward,
going against those cirrocumuli
and the blue void;
third, that above the mountains covered with larches
you, dark atmospheric sea cucumbers,
are all too brazen,
now disappearing, now transmogrifying yourselves
into all sorts of lascivious lights and forms.
To summarize all this,
soft dubious nimbus,
although you allow me to enjoy several chinks of sensuous sunlight,
although you send me rude fragrance in the wind,
your intention cast out in the entire sky
with your gray black wings and tentacles,
your fluid mass of great baritone,
is too evident to hide.
Therefore, I, a humble official,
considering all the positions I occupy, public and private,
give you, these last moments,
a glare brimming with outrage,
ready to leave this summit
promptly, yes promptly.

▪ 6 / 1 / 1 9 2 7 ▪

AT THE VERY END of the blue sky,
above the atmospheric strata where even hydrogen is too thin,
there lives a group of eternal, transparent living things
who'd find it too cloying
to think even such thoughts as:
"I am the entirety of this world.
The world is the shadow of a transient, blue dream."

• 6/12/1927 •

RAVING

My sin has turned to illness,
I am helpless
sleeping in the valley sky.

At least at least
onto this body fever
this year's blue spear blades, take root.
Out of this humid air,
rain, be born
and moisten the drought earth.

• 6/13/1927 •

COLLEAGUES

In those days when I had my desk
among yours, in this square room,
if on a bright calm afternoon like this
        . . . In the window, an acacia branch sways . . .
someone happened to visit us
with different ideas or dressed differently,
we would merely exchange casual looks,
faint expressions meaningless even to ourselves
        . . . The summer clouds collapse and shine . . .
but today, tired and weak after avoiding
the wasted fields and the villagers' fierce eyes,
foolishly, foolishly longing
for yesterday's comfortable address
when I enter this square room
your words and looks
become ten times as strong as your thoughts
        . . . The wind burns . . .
and strike me
        . . . The wind burns, grain stalks burn . . .

                    • 7 / 1 / 1 9 2 7 •

A RICE-GROWING EPISODE

Look, that paddy,
there's too much nitrogen for that kind of rice
so now we cut the water off

and don't do a third weeding
        . . . He came running along the ridges.
                Wiping his sweat in green paddies, still a child . . .
Do you have any phosphate left?
You've used it all?
OK, if we have the same weather
for five more days,
pluck off all those
drooping leaves,
you see, leaves drooping like these
        . . . He nods repeatedly, wiping at his sweat.
                When he came to my winter lectures,
                though he had already worked a year
                he still had a bright smile like an apple.
                Now he's tanned with sun and sweat
                and looks gaunt after many sleepless nights . . .
And also
if at the end of this month
those stalks grow higher than your chest,
use the top button on your shirt as a measure
and cut all the leaf tips above it
        . . . Not only the sweat
                he's wiping his tears too . . .
I have already looked at the paddy
you planned yourself.
About the Riku-u No. 132[34]

34. A species of rice developed in 1921 to better withstand plant diseases, insects, and cold weather by Terao Hiroshi at the Riku'u Agricultural Station, of the Ministry of Agriculture and Forestry, in Akita.

you did a very fine job.
The fertilizing was good and even,
and they are growing sturdily.
You used the ammonium sulfate too, didn't you?
They may say lots of things
but there's no worry about that paddy.
Four bushels per quarter acre,
that we can be sure of.
Keep on with it.
For you, true learning from now on
doesn't mean to follow dutifully
those who teach as a business and then play tennis.
Yours is the kind of learning
etched into yourself
in the blizzards, in the sparse free time between work,
crying —
which will soon sprout vigorously
and no one knows how big it will grow.
That's the beginning of new knowledge.
Now I must go. Take care.
　　　. . . May the transparent power
　　　　　of clouds and winds
　　　　　　be transferred
　　　　　　to the child . . .

· 7/10/1927 ·

FLOOD

Under the malicious glints of the clouds
the Kitakami, grown twice in width, perhaps ten times in volume,
bears yellow waves.
All the iron barges are being tugged to the army camp.
A motorboat sputters.
The water flowing back from downstream
has already turned into marshes
the paddies on the dried riverbed,
hidden the bean fields,
and devastated half the mulberries.
Gleaming like a snail's trail
it has made an island of the grass patch under the pines
and of the Chinese cabbage fields.
When and how they got there I don't know
but on the warm frightening beach
several dark figures stand, afloat.
One holds a fishnet.
I recognize Hōsuke in leggings.
Has the water already
robbed us of our autumn food?
I climb the roof to look.
I hauled all the manure bundles to a high place.
As for the plows and baskets
I went in the water a few minutes ago, up to my waist,
and managed to retrieve them.

• 8/15/1927 •

THE MASTER OF THE FIELD

Through the fallen rice stalks and miscanthus,
across the water glistening white,
under the thunder and clouds,
master, I come to visit you
and find you sitting formally on the veranda,
listening to the movements of the sky and the field.
For seventy years,
every day, at daybreak and sunset,
you have cut mountains of grass,
you have worn handwoven hemp even in winter,
so now your back is rounder than the pine trunk,
your fingers are crumpled up,
your forehead is etched with diagrams
of the rains, the suns, and the hardships,
and your eyes are hollower than the caves.
Every phase of the field and sky
has a duplicate copy in you,
and the direction of its change
and its influences on the crops
are muttered in your throat
as if they were the words of the wind.
And yet, today, your face is so bright!
After two thousand fertilizing plans
completed in the hope of rich harvest,
it is about time the flowers opened
pushing out of the ears of rice stalks,
but the fierce rain that lasted four days
and the thunder and rain since this morning

have felled the rice stalks in many places.
I think that tomorrow or the day after
if only they see the sun, they will all rise,
and we'll probably get the crop we expected.
If not, all these villages will have to face
another dark winter.
Against the thunder and the rain
I find words useless
and can only stand in silence.
Above the pines and willows
streaks of clouds trail,
and the gray water overflows
the banks reinforced so many times.
Nevertheless, the easy brightness on your face
bears no trace of the feeling you gave,
the year before last, looking at the summer sky
that had brought the drought.
Now, with the confidence you have given me
I am about to visit the village again.
As I leave, I see on your forehead
a cloud of uncertainty float up
and clear in a moment.
What it meant, I could never guess
even if I thought and thought,
going through a hundred possibilities,
but, dear master,
if it has to do with me,
even though my knowledge, all secondhand, is scanty,
even though I am as frivolous as a bird,
dear master, please look me straight in the eye

as intently as you can,
please listen to my breathing
as carefully as you can.
I wear old Western suits made of white hemp
and carry a torn Western umbrella made of silk,
but I am determined
to protect with my life
the Juryōbon[35] of the Lotus Sutra
which, by the blessings of all the buddhas and bodhisattvas,
you recite each morning.
And now, dear master,
what heavenly drums reverberate!
what purity of light!
I bow silently
and bid you farewell.

• 3/28/1927 •

THE BREEZE COMES FILLING THE VALLEY

Ah
from the south, and from the southwest,
the breeze comes filling the valley,
dries my shirt soaked with sweat,
cools my hot forehead and eyelids.

35. Chapter 16: "The Lifetime of the Tathagata" (Gene Reeves, unpublished translation), "The Life Span of Thus Come One" (Burton Watson, *The Lotus Sutra* [New York: Columbia University Press, 1993]).

Stirring the field of rice stalks that have risen,
shaking the dark raindrops from each blade,
the breeze comes filling the valley.
As a result of all kinds of hardship,
the July rice, bifurcating,
foretold a fruitful autumn,
but by mid-August
twelve red daybreaks
and six days of 90 percent humidity
made the stalks weak and long,
and though they put on ears and flowers
the fierce rain yesterday
felled them one after another.
Here, in the driving sheets of rain,
a fog, cold as if mourning,
covered the fallen rice.
Having suffered all of the bad conditions,
few of which we thought we'd have.
they showed the worst result we'd expected,
but then,
when we thought all the odds were against their rising,
because of the slight differences in seedling preparation
and in the use of superphosphate,
all the stalks are up today.
And I had expected this,
and to tell you of this early recovery
I looked for you,
but you avoided me.
The rain grew harder

until it flooded this ground.
There was no sign of clearing.
Finally, like a crazy man
I ran out in the rain,
telephoned the weather bureau,
went from village to village, asking for you,
until, hoarse,
in the terrible lightning,
I went home late at night.
But in the end I did not sleep.
And, look,
this morning the east, the golden rose, opens,
the clouds, the beacons, rise one after another,
the high-voltage wires roar,
the stagnant fog runs in the distance.
The rice stalks have risen at last.
They are living things,
precision machines.
All stand erect.
At their tips, which waited patiently in the rain,
tiny white flowers glisten
and above the quiet amber puddles reflecting the sun
red dragonflies glide.
Ah, we must dance, dance like children,
and that's not enough.
If they fall again,
they will decidedly rise again.
If, as they have,
they can stand humidity like this,

every village is certain to get
five bushels a quarter acre.
From the horizon buried beneath a forest,
from the row of dead volcanoes shining blue,
the wind comes across the rice paddies,
makes the chestnut leaves glitter.
Now, the fresh evaporation,
the transparent movement of sap.
Ah, in the middle of this plain,
in the middle of these rice paddies rustling as powerfully
as if they were reeds,
we must dance, clapping our hands, like the innocent gods of
the past,
and that is not enough.

· 7/14/1927 ·

WHAT A COWARD I am.
Because the rain at daybreak
beat down the rice stalks around here,
I work like mad,
I try to distract myself from the fear.
But look, again in the west
the black death floats up.
In the spring, in the spring,
was that not bright love itself?

· 8/20/1927 ·

NO MATTER WHAT he does, it's too late,
he's one of our ordinary friends.
He reads magazines, raises rabbits,
makes all the cages himself,
puts twenty or so of them under the lean-to,
and their eyes are moist and red,
they eat cowpeas from your hand,
they even chirp like warblers.
And that too is too late.
No matter what he does, it's too late,
he's one of our ordinary friends.
He looks at catalogs, marks them,
gets gladiolas by mail,
plants them with labels
before a patch of *myōga*[36] and a camellia,
and large flowers bloom, glaringly,
the old people say they're divine,
passersby all praise them.
And that too is too late.
No matter what he does, it's too late,
he's one of our ordinary friends.
He buys mushroom spores,
clears the shed,
even makes a compost of wheat straw,
hangs a thermometer,
pours water every day,

36. A species of ginger whose young stalk and "flower" are prized for their use as a spice.

and soon white champignons
poke out their faces one after another.
And that too is too late.
No matter what he does, it's too late,
he's one of our ordinary friends.
He puts on tortoiseshell rubber boots,
buys and wears an olive crepe shirt.
His cheeks are bright, hair kinky and pretty.
Still, for all that,
no matter what he does, it's too late,
no matter what he does, it's too late,
he's one of our ordinary friends,
he's one of our ordinary friends.

• 8/20/1927 •

IMPRESSIONS OF AN EXHIBITION
OF FLOATING-WORLD PAINTINGS

Glue and a small amount of alum
        . . . oh, network of billions of such
            supermicroscopic delicate precise dots . . .
connect the snow-white tapa fibers
and form a fragile rectangular membrane
which increases or decreases sensitively with the humidity,
and breathes subtly, subtly with the temperature
    there
    etched suggestively are

snow-fleshed or ivory-colored half-nude statues
dyed lovingly are
the nine monochromes
as the light shifts
they collapse feebly and fade
Look at these cheeks from a time long past
which now brim with insoluble smiles,
now transfuse too soluble passions
up to the slender eyes.
In the square brown-tiled room,
on the walls above the brown rug,
they hung like windows peering into the enormous
four-dimensional orbits.
The refined ladies and gentlemen of the Kingdom of Japan
endowed with religious beliefs of high grace and elegance
and with hereditary taste
stroll modestly oh so modestly
in each of the small paper spaces
none exceeding twelve square decimeters.
They purify, in that distant time and space,
the flames which too gentle models of lust
incite in their hearts,
and come and go lightly, eyebrows nobly raised.
They close the gap of time and space
and return in an instant to the paper
where breathing the fragrance of old desires
they pass by, absentminded, light-footed.

There, the apple-green rich grassland,
the full water reflecting the thinly clouded sky,
the red torii shining small in the distance,
and the rows of decorative *chrysocolla* cedars.

　　Creators of the everlasting divine nation
　　Greatest authors of children's stories told visually

In the heavy, stagnant air
the wind is wearying,
and the woman, too sensual,
standing on the hilltop, throws one, two, three
porcelain cups, which leave slight ripples
upon the viscid yellow waves.
And here, each ripple
is a great event.
In response appears
a white cloud, dazzling for the first time
and moves around the yellow hill
dotted with tiny pines.

　　Designer of a different *atmosphere*
　　and an innocent setting
In the autumn
they too thresh grain and cereal
and pull the clappers,
but with them the freezing point is fifty Fahrenheit,
the snow is cotton stacked up by the wind,
and when it piles up on wavy willows

it must do so by quite a different gravity.
In the summer, the rain does fall
from the black sky;
yet their leaf boats are moved
not so much by the wind as by their curiosity.
The water lilies are all of the kind called Lotus
and when they open, they make the evening air
tremble like a drum.

Such childhood soon turns
into burning dazzling youth,
and the eyes loaded with rich love dance
and the quiet bones and muscles squeak.

Red fireworks, the water gleaming in the distance,
red lips inviting as,
for example, raw tuna,
and around their eyes
a faint white of shyness
which may be on a wind's shadow
or may be what the paper has exuded.
Wanton eyebrows shaven blue.
Beneath the sharp second-day moon
their eyes, tired and dimmed,
reflect the gray roofs of the town.

The wind descends from the black sky,
the willow sways,
and lust flickers after the wind.

• 6/15/1928 •

IN THE LEADEN moonlight
the enormous pine branches
lying here and there on the ground
might be mistaken for green rhinoceroses.
The recent sleet scraped
and thrashed them down
from the large treetops above.
The enormous shadows of the pine rows
and the moon-white net covering the grassland —
over there on the frozen riverbed
a naked baby was found abandoned.
From the cliff top village
a suspect was led off,
the people petitioned —
that seems long ago.
Exactly a month later
before the frozen February daybreak
a woman crying wildly
calling a name
ran down the cliff to the river.
It must be the mother, pulled by the baby
to the river, I thought,
jumped out of bed and opened the door.
Then I heard a man catch up
and come back, soothing her.
The woman sobbed as she came
through the frozen mulberry field.
That much I could tell.
Then silence.
That seems even earlier.

Now the snow has all but vanished.
The river, gray as the sky,
glides south silently.
In the east, at Gorin Pass, curled winds
and syrupy clouds about to burst into tears
overhang, their hems vague, curled.
On this side, just above the dark river
plovers move along upstream.
How many times were you born? How many times frozen to death?
so they seem to sing.
Upstream, a haze white as wax,
and mountain forms are invisible.
From beneath the vague red light of town
the sound of a dog frantically barking —
the winds roar through the pines
again in cold broken rhythm.

THE THIRD ART

I was making ridges for turnips
and a small person with white hair
was standing behind me, I noticed.
What are you going to sow, he asked.
I'm going to sow red turnips, I replied.
Don't make ridges for red turnips like that.
He held out his hand quietly,
took my hoe, and raked
one part of the ridge aslant.

My head, hushed, rang,
and as though thoroughly drugged,
I just stood there, stunned.
The sun shone, the wind blew,
our shadows lay on the sand,
and the river over there gleamed.
But I, utterly in bliss, wondered
what brush stroke for ink painting,
what fragrance of a sculptor's chisel
could be superior to this.

THE LANDOWNER

When water rumbles
and birds, flock after flock,
float against the dazzling clouds and smoke in the east
and pass above the small pine field,
the man, liquor-bleared eyes red as agates,
wearing cattail leggings,
an old Snider slung across his back,
arms crossed high on his chest,
wanders alone like an angry ghost.
In the thin strip of a mountainside village,
just because he has 7.5 acres of field,
everyone looks on him as a lord
and in fact he himself, though up to his neck in debt,
puts on the dignified airs of a landowner.
Behind him, continuous from the foot

of the Owl Wood and Mount Hexagon
extends an enormous hill, three miles square,
where chestnut trees, not yet budding,
gather their brown tops in tight congregation
and below it,
in the moonlight-colored grassland,
stands in the Oriental fashion
a wood of magnificent alder trees.
In such a pink spring,
his head sunk deeply on his chest,
the man wanders alone, desolate.
Because the rent rice he gets
is all borrowed again by autumn
(There's nothing left to eat, they say,
as they plead with him by turns)
he declares, Like a man
I'll feed myself on my own,
and goes off with his old Snider.
But when he manages to haul back a bear,
they say, "He killed the mountain god
so this year's crop is poor."
Though now the rice nursery adds to the green gold each morning,
the ferns along the ridges open their buds,
horsetails shine blue,
and here and everywhere
the people raise their tired arms
and plow dry paddies
with three-pronged spades that glitter,
he no longer knows whether
he should shoot a bear

or what other thing,
and, his eyes bleared, red,
paces back and forth like an angry ghost.

HATEFUL KUMA EATS HIS LUNCH

Facing the glistening river,
eating lunch by himself —
that's Kuma, no less.
Since I moved alone
into that abandoned shack,
he's been going as far as town to say,
"A ghost comes out of the woods"
Or, "A Woman visits him every night."
He's that hateful Kuma, no less.
But today, it's not his game.
First, while sitting on the grass,
intently devouring his food,
he allows an enemy who hasn't once revenged himself
to pass behind him.
Second, he doesn't have his usual advantage,
my obstacle, which is mass psychology.
Under the azure, we are definitely one to one.
Third, he's vented enough resentment already
and has little hatred left.
So I feel sorry for him
and would like to avoid him
but if I did, he'd think I ran away.

This consideration compels me
to win today.
The river glistens,   ·
and downstream, there's a noise of boats.
Kuma sits by a pine stump
shaped like a small table.
He turns and gives me a rude glance.
Then he gets so upset, really upset!
The yellow chopsticks he holds limply —
he opens them about 40 degrees
and with one of them
pokes at the rice stuffed in his mouth.
And of course I pass behind him.
Now behind me
the generalissimo is perhaps too excited
to taste anything as he goes on eating rice.
But I have won in so clear-cut a manner,
I feel dark blue, feel it's no good,
though I haven't done anything special.
He sowed the seeds as suited him,
he reaped the crop as suited him.

SINCE THE DOCTOR is still young,
they say he doesn't mind jumping out of bed at night,
discounts drugs for them, and doesn't do
complicated things like injections
or anything that desecrates nature too much.
I think that's why they like him.

By the time this doctor finally comes to feel
just as the villagers do,
and work as an integral part,
he'll have fallen behind in new techniques
and at the lecture of the county doctors' society
he'll curl up small, a perpetual listener.
Such is the effect of this sunlight,
water, and the transparent air.
Every time I pass here by train,
I try to imagine what kind of person he is.
Because, presiding over this beautiful clinic,
he has a face like a chameleon,
I feel very sorry for him.
Four or five persons have bowed.
Now the doctor quietly returns the bow.

NIGHT

When with hot palms, unable to sleep,
people still have had some sleep, from the old days,
gripping a crumpled towel,
or holding a black clay-slate stone.

A FEW more times
I must glare at Kōsuke.
In the stinging wind from the snow-covered mountain

he decreed that the entire village turn out,
had a jumble of cedars and chestnuts cut,
had them erected,
two by the willow near the canal,
three along the cliff at the end of the woods,
those totally unnecessary electric poles
for totally unnecessary lights.
And now he says we'll have a completion ceremony
with the double aim of thanking the linemen,
he says we'll drink in the woods,
he says only the bosses will drink,
he says I'm one of the bosses.
Damn it! I'm not one of you bastards,
who trudge all day in a lazy pack
pretending to play truly important roles,
and instead of really trying to work
put on a show, saying
"The hole's too shallow," "The pole's warped."
Donning his sooty boater carefully in this weather,
wearing baggy white pants like a silk dealer,
he's making a fire in the woods — such an ugly man.
I'll be damned if I won't go up to him
and glare at him again.
Yet, though I wouldn't mind glaring,
the cold wind with rain
hurts my eyes so.
Besides, for the last few minutes
Kōsuke has been trying hard to please me.
When I glare at him he deliberately blinks his eyes.
And his nose is black, I don't know why.

It may be that my anger comes
from my innate hatred of labor
and the fact that I haven't been feeling well since I came to
     the village;
because I don't know what to do about it,
now that Kōsuke has accepted the electric company's offer
and schemed a project like this,
I pour it all on him
the way supersaturated vapor
with tiny dust particles for a base
turns into rain.
Come to think of it,
the electric poles are not that unnecessary.
In fact, when I first came here
I wondered why the hell
they didn't have a single lamp.
Anyway, it isn't as easy as you might think
to glare at someone
when the wind is this cold
and the blue pungent smoke from Kōsuke's fire
hits me right in the face.
Two bottles of sake and five pieces of bean curd.
Kyūji, who lives near the woods,
brought the plates, soy sauce, and chopsticks.
The birches let their yellow leaves fly about,
the cedars drop brown needles.
Of the six linemen sent by the company
only one remains, like a hostage,
trying to get warm from the blue smoke.
Kōsuke didn't tell the others anything,

even the foreman, as they left,
but captured this one lingering, left behind,
like a specimen,
to give the appearance of "thanking the linemen."
As he tries hard to stir up the fire
and gives words of thanks to him,
the lineman squats, ill at ease,
his dirty white hair straggling down
from his red-banded cap,
his Adam's apple risen to an unusual height.
The wind blows, blows from the west,
the cedars shake, red leaves of birches fall noisily.
Well, anyway, I'll join them.
But I will accept neither sake nor bean curd.
I will simply warm my hands over the fire
and glare at Kōsuke as fiercely as I can.
Then when I'm done I'll leave at once.

A HORSE

carefully wearing a load of rice
comes, with all its strength,
crossing a gleaming, shallow river in a blizzard.
The man as well
carrying on his back the wood of about ten pine trees
comes trudging, looking down.
From Horse Head to Table
the mountains make a row of white,
grass patches, woods and all.

Above, the sky pale, clear,
blows down, head-on,
a dry cold wind
which might be called a freezing sirocco,
and one is tempted to feel
the pale-gleaming sky is one's enemy.
Carrying an umbrella-shaped wood on his back,
thinking, A harvest of sixty loads instead of fifty
wouldn't make life a lot easier,
he comes quietly across the blizzard,
a resigned smile
on his lips shaped like lotus petals.
The horse, hair all splattered,
drenched with sweat,
plods on, blown by the blizzard.

A YOUNG LAND CULTIVATION DEPARTMENT
TECHNICIAN'S RECITATIVE ON IRISES

Again separating myself
from the surveying group
I have come back over the beautiful green highlands
visiting on the way
dozens of dense, sensuous clusters of purple,
gatherings of irises fragrant in the sun.
To carry around pointed transits
and striped poles
trying to compete with ancient Kitakami for age,

to cut railways and paddies
and chip rocks
from a section of the semiplain
that has stored days since the Cretaceous Period
only to turn out two maps —
that, under the azure vault,
is unequivocally the Original Sin.
Tomorrow, quivering motors
and huge plows shining dull
will bury under countless grooves
of overturned black earth
hundreds of these tall
pliant flower stalks
and each one of these petals and pistils
that look like silk or blue wax.
Then they will become dreary humus
and in time help grow coarse tough corn
and ears of oats,
but I, along with this clear south wind,
cannot but give the flowers
all my helpless caresses and boundless love.

THE MAN I parted from, below,
still with his brown horse behind him,
walks away along the bank,
trailing puffs of tobacco smoke.
This morning he hadn't smoked
but as he came to the mountain flats

the air began to warm and shine
and maybe he felt relaxed enough
to enjoy a puff.
For that matter, even the horse
seems to be limping, just as a joke.
The other side, refreshing summer grass stretches
down to Ubaishi and Takahi
and the light brown firelines
that hedge in at distinct right angles
make the highlands look
like a dozen or more playing cards spread out.
And there pass one after another
deep dark-blue shadows of clouds
and the aquamarine legs of winds.
The face of one of the cards
begins to brighten from one edge
and produces what look like
glittering red ants.
They are pasture horses turned loose.
The entire picture violently shakes again in heat haze.
The horses glisten, perhaps because
they twitch their chests
or flick themselves with their tails.
At the other end, facing the horses,
a man in white pants
with a small bush on his back
shakes terribly like everything else.
It's eleven o'clock in the morning
and he must be giving salt to the horses.
Many of them gather there.

If the smoking man's brown horse joins them
they might tell him, "You're too late, buddy.
We're done with today's special treat."
Or perhaps horses don't say things like that
but only feel them vaguely
along with the warmth of light and wind.
Bees buzz around me.
The crag where I stand and enjoy this perspective
grows faintly warm.
The west lies beyond the layers of hills.
In the Kitakami valley
gray mist collects and stagnates.
Above its upper edge, far in the north,
what looks indigo and monstrous
must be thawing Iwate Volcano.
Right below it, at its foot,
Numamori and Numamoridaira
have exactly the same topography as this area.
And oh, when I stand alone on the lithosphere,
beneath a blue sky like this,
I feel a mysterious, helpless
love for our land.
Another cloud shadow takes over
and the herd of horses darkens.
The smoking man still clops on with his horse
going slowly along the great pathway
on the deserted flats.

KOREANS PASS, DRUMMING

For ten days after I came down with pneumonia
during daytime too I was asleep almost in bliss
waking I couldn't even breathe
couldn't even move my body a little
but in exhausted sleep
I was moving freely
over a large mountain covered white with snow
along its rocky path
carrying yellow triangular banners
and spears adorned with bird feathers
in single file an army comes

PNEUMONIA

This blue-dark enormous room —
how could this be my lungs?
in it sulking elementary schoolteachers
carrying on a grudgy conference for four hours already
pump the pump on its part makes rackety noise
arms and legs I don't even know where they are

none of these things seems mine anymore
except it's me who manages to think like this
damn it! thinking's just thinking
how the hell do you know it's you?
well then do you mean I don't exist. . . .
oh shit! don't start that now

AH that
please don't say that tonight
please don't say that tonight please
with my lungs half burnt up
barely barely
I exhale carbonic acid
and welcome a little bit of oxygen
how could I decide it now
ah that is something
healthy ten years' thinking
can't grasp
if the bomb
bursts snow-white in my head
the fierce heat that boils up there
and the bad gas that freezes the blood
no longer will I be able either to spew out
or to wash away

It's no use[37]
it won't stop
see it's welling up in gulps
since last night I haven't slept and the blood keeps coming out
around me it's blue and hushed
somehow I feel I'll die soon
but what a fine wind
because it's almost Clear Brightness[38]
the clean wind comes to us
as if swelling up and out of the blue sky
setting young maple shoots and hairlike flowers
into the wavy motion of autumn grass
even the mats of rush with burn scars look blue
I don't know if you're on your way back from a doctors' meeting
wearing a black frock coat like that
and so sincere in giving me various treatments
now even if I die I'll make no complaint
for all the bleeding
I feel untroubled and no pain
because I suppose the soul has half left the body
except because of the blood
I can't tell you this & I feel terrible
you look at me & I must be a disastrous sight

---

37. This poem describes the result of a blood-stanching operation that Kenji underwent to address a gum problem he developed in the late spring of 1932.

38. In Japanese, *Seimei* (or in Chinese, *qingming*): By the lunar calendar, in which the year is divided into twenty-four segments, this is the fifteenth day after the spring equinox, or April 4 or 5 by the solar calendar.

but I see only
the blue sky that's still clean
and the transparent wind.

PAST NOON it's three o'clock
and in my stricken left lung
a muddy red fire catches on
then the rain fierce ceaseless
at first hot and dark and
soon dazzling the rain
washing cedar and *sakaki*[39]
falls until daybreak comes

WHEN that terrifying black cloud
again comes to seize me
I writhe alone, helpless & hot
I'll wed that rain cloud
covering the Kitakami river valley I said
I long for that alluvial plateau
carrying both woods and grass fields on it
I sent word to people half as a joke
half eager truly thought that
the blue mountain and river as they were
were my own self I thought

39. An evergreen glabrous tree whose leafy twigs are used in Shinto rites.

ah that torments me
when amid pain of illness and sweat
those swirling black clouds
and the Prussian-blue horizon
again come up close to my eyes
I writhe alone, helpless & hot
ah father mother younger brother
after all the favors and kindnesses
how can I
throw my body
to that terrifying black cloud
ah friends distant friend
do you know of this terrifying other mien
of the dazzling dome
transparent winds grass fields and forests

THUMP THUMP THUMP thump thump[40]
thump thump thump thump thump
being beaten down   thump
being beaten down   thump
pitch-dark in seaweed   thump thump thump
a sea of salt   thump thump thump thump

40. A large part of this poem depends on the sound effects of the three recurring Chinese characters in Japanese pronunciation: *chō,* here given as "thump"; *son,* "song"; and *satsu,* "sat." Of the three, *chō,* which originally meant "nail," is, when repeated as *chōchō,* used to represent a variety of sounds: an ax cutting a tree, swords striking at each other, the call of a bird, the pouring rain. The character for *son* means "respect," "reverence," and that for *satsu* means "kill."

fever　　thump thump thump thump

fever fever　　thump thump thump

(song song sat sat sat

sat sat song song song

song song sat sat sat

sat sat song song song)

genie　　you've finally told the truth

try it　　thump thump thump

you can never beat me dammit

the shadow of some giant bird

huh　　thump thump thump

sea pale white dawn　　thump

in the vigorously rising steam

fragrantly breathing I miss

there's that bud of a giant flower

DESPERATELY trying to sleep to sleep

I remain in cold sweat and fever

the clock points to four o'clock

I as if talking to myself

envy me at four o'clock yesterday

ah at the time

I'd forgotten sweat and pain

was back in my light heart and body of twenty

and through the sepia stand of trees

in the clean early-winter air

together with a group of stonecutters

I was climbing Ōsawazaka Pass

WIND IS CALLING me out in front,
"Come, get up,
put on your red shirt
and the usual tattered overcoat
and quickly come out to the front."
Winds are by turns shouting,
"To welcome you when you are out
we are all
thrashing sidewise
the particles of sleep you like.
You jump out quickly
and above the ragged rock over there,
in the leafless black woods,
marry, as you promised,
one of us who has
a beautiful soprano voice,"
repeatedly, repeatedly,
so are the winds shouting out in front.

MY CHEST now
is a hot sad salt lake
along its coast for two hundred miles
a grove of coal-black lepidodendron goes on and on
and why on earth
do I have to remain laid up
still, without moving
until reptiles change into some bird shape

WHEN I OPEN my eyes an April wind
crumbles down toward me from the lazuline sky
and the maple spreads its young faintly red shoots
fully across the window.
The blood from last evening still doesn't stop
and everyone is gazing into me.

Not knowing who it is that vomits
that which wells up again, lukewarm,
I sleep, blue and blue.
What now passes over my forehead
is a line of clean, clear wind
atop that dead volcano.

NIGHT

So far for two hours
the blood from my throat hasn't stopped.
Outside people walk no longer,
trees quietly breathing and budding this spring night.
This very place is the training ground[41] of spring, the bodhisattva
    has abandoned a billion of his bodies,
various buddhas live here in nirvana, and so
tonight, now, here, seen by no one,
I can die alone —

41. *Dōjō* (Sanskrit, *bodhi-manda*): the place of enlightenment, or the Way.

I've decided on this thought many times,
I have told it to myself,
but again lukewarm
new blood wells up and
once again pale-white I become frightened.

• 4/28/1929 •

WHILE ILL

why on earth is this?
breathing gradually became shorter
now completely stopped
having stopped it's suffocating
do you mean to inhale breath deliberately
      . . . the room is full of snow light . . .
you managed to inhale breath
it becomes shorter again
it's a fine geometrical progress
the common ratio to be sure is three-quarters
            sleepy
                  sleepy
                        sleepy
if you fall asleep because it's sleepy you will die
exactly stir up your effort
absolutely eyes! eyes!! eyes!!! open 'em
yessir

once again breathe extremely deeply
again a geometrical progression is it?
this is no good
there's no time to part with anyone
sleep now
go ahead and sleep
no it's no time to sleep
stir up
open your eyes
put your hands on your chest and inhale breath
    . . . mother's in the kitchen the sound of water . . .

AND IT MUST be that I will die soon
but what on earth is what is called I
I thought rethought it a number of times read and read
heard it was this was taught it was that
but in the end it isn't clear yet
what is called I. . . .

I shall die soon
today or tomorrow.
Again, anew, I contemplate: What am I?
I am ultimately nothing other than a principle.
My body is bones, blood, flesh,
which are in the end various molecules,
combinations of dozens of atoms;
the atom is in the end a form of vacuum,
and so is the external world.
The principle by which I sense my body and the external world thus
and by which these materials work in various ways
is called I.
The moment I die and return to the vacuum,
the moment I perceive myself again,
in both times, what is there is only a single principle.
The name of that original law is called *The Lotus Sutra of the
Wonderful Law,* they say.
All this, because one wants bodhi, one believes the bodhisattva.
By believing the bodhisattva, one believes the Buddha.
Various buddhas are in countless billions, and the Buddha is also the
law.
The original law for the various buddhas is yes *The Lotus Sutra of
the Wonderful Law.*
I am devoted to *The Lotus Sutra of the Wonderful Law.*
Life, too, is the life of *The Wonderful Law.*
Death, too, is the death of *The Wonderful Law.*
From this body to the buddha body I shall uphold it well.

Midnight I wake with a start[42]
and listen. Downstairs, on the west side,
ah, that child
    coughs and cries,
        again coughs and
                cries.
In the intervals
I constantly hear her mother try
softly to persuade,
                try to soothe her.
That room is a cold room.
During the day no sun shines in,
during the night, drafts come in
                through the floorboards.
In December, the third year of Shōwa,
    when I in that room
        had acute
            pneumonia
the child's newly married father and mother
gave me this large
        sunny room of theirs

42. In translating "October 20th," "(October) 28," and "November 3rd," I have retained the original line formations as best I could; I have also italicized them because Kenji used *katakana* instead of the usual *hiragana*. Early on the Japanese developed these two types of phonetic writing systems out of Chinese characters. During certain periods *katakana* was regarded as masculine and mechanical, while *hiragana* was regarded as feminine and literary. Since the Second World War, *hiragana* has been the main vehicle for Japanese, with *katakana* reserved for onomatopoeia and foreign words.

and moved down there,
        that dark room
                where I had lain for four months.
And in February
        that child was born
                there.
For a girl she had
                a brave heart,
stumbling or falling,
        that sort of thing
                would not make her
                        cry.
Last year
        when I finally recovered
and began growing morning glories and chrysanthemums,
she would water them with me,
        sometimes
                cut off
                        the stalks with buds.
Toward the end of this past September again
I fell ill in Tokyo.
I had
        expected to die there,
but when again my parents' compassion
                helped me to return,
she welcomed me, smiling by the gate,
and then from the staircase
        shouted at the top of her voice,
        You've been gone a long time!
Now because of her fever, panting,

she doesn't know how to put her mind in order;
though one night
she said, I don't know,
                and slept well,
tonight she just
            just coughs and
                    cries.
Ah, Mahābrahamn, tonight in spite of myself
I am disturbed
            and humbly plead with you:
Though she is three,
she has stood upright, joined her hands,
and recited the opening of the Lotus Sutra.
            No matter what her sins in a former life,
may her illness, her pain,
            be transferred to me.

• (1931) •

(OCTOBER) 28

        I do not want
                    pleasure
        I do not want
                    fame
now I just
        wish to offer
                offer
        this base useless body

to the Lotus Sutra
to light
    a speck of dust
and if forgiven
    become
        servant to father and mother
to return their billions
    of favors
ill and faced with death
    I have no other
       wish

UNTITLED

Neither rain
nor wind
nor snow nor summer's heat
will affect his robust body.
Free of anger
and desire
he will always keep a calm smile.
A quart of brown rice, miso
and some vegetables will be his daily food.
In all things
he will not think of himself
but will observe, hear, and understand well
and will not forget.
Living in a small, reed-thatched hut

under pine trees in the field,
he will go to tend
a sick child in the east
or carry a bundle of rice plants
for a tired mother in the west
or try to dispel the fear
of a dying man in the south
or stop a trivial quarrel or lawsuit
of people in the north.
He will shed tears if a drought comes
and trudge disconsolately if the summer is cold.
Called a bum by all
he will be praised by no one
and will bother no one.
I should like to become
such a man.

• TRANSLATED BY MAKOTO UEDA •

NOVEMBER 3RD

neither yielding to rain
nor yielding to wind
yielding neither to
snow nor to summer heat
           with a stout body
                   like that
without greed

never getting angry
always smiling quiet-
             ly
eating one and a half pints of brown rice
 and bean paste and a bit of
                  vegetables a day
in everything
not taking oneself
            into account
               looking listening understanding well
and not forgetting
living in the shadow of pine trees in a field
 in a small
            hut thatched with miscanthus
if in the east there's a
             sick child
going and nursing
              him
if in the west there's a tired mother
going and carrying
      for her
      bundles of rice
if in the south
      there's someone
               dying
going
 and saying
      you don't have to be
        afraid

if in the north
      there's a quarrel
             or a lawsuit
saying it's not worth it
              stop it
in a drought
      shedding tears
in a cold summer
      pacing back and forth lost
called
      a good-for-nothing
          by everyone
neither praised
nor thought a pain
      someone
          like that
is what I want
      to be

▪ (1 9 3 1) ▪

(Last Poems)

Within these ten square miles: is this in Hinuki alone?
The rice ripe and for three festival days
                    the whole sky clear

Because of an illness, crumbling,
                         this life —
if I could give it for the dharma
               how glad I would be

• (9/21/1933) •

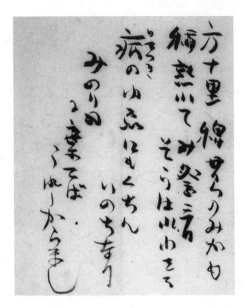

The last tanka written by Kenji;
he wrote them just before his death
on September 21, 1933.

FOUR IMAGES

TANIKAWA SHUNTARŌ

IMAGE I

Printed on the flyleaf, in soft reddish-yellow like that of whetting powder, is the picture. In a *zashiki*[1] of an old house in the countryside are small children dressed in kimonos too short for them, dancing hand in hand. Written horizontally on the picture mold near the ceiling[2] is "Round the Highways" — is that the name of the dance? In one corner, separate from the ring of dancers, is a single child; he seems to have something in his hand, but I can't tell what it is. An elementary school boy myself, I know the child is a *zashiki bokko*.[3]

Isn't it odd, though? I wonder. "There was not one that the others didn't know, there was not a single face that was the same as any other," and there were supposed to be "exactly ten children," though "no matter how you counted, there were eleven of them." Then you aren't supposed to be able to tell who the *zashiki bokko* is, right? Once you know who the *zashiki bokko* is, the *zashiki bokko* ceases to be one. I, a child, despise the illustrator a little. His name is Yokoi Kōzō. He writes this in his afterword:

"Readers, I had the honor of receiving a request to draw pictures for the cover and illustrations for this book. I am truly happy and

2 2 5

grateful that I was selected from among many painters. Miyazawa Sensei was a world-class genius teller of children's stories that Japan produced, and a man of admirable character. A man of character is someone who does good things without cause." This is a wonderful piece of writing by someone absorbed in his work. His illustrations are wonderful, too, as I look at them now.

The Biography of Gusukō Budori,[4] published in April 1941 by Haneda Shoten. On the list of publications following the colophon are books such as *The Law to Protect Secrets on Resources for Military Use* and *The Law to Protect Military Secrets.*

IMAGE 11

On the back of the box for the book is written, also in Yokoi Kōzō's hand, that famous statement:

> Unless the entire world
> becomes
> happy, there can be no happiness
> for individuals.
> —*Miyazawa Kenji*

The statement was too proper for me, and I reacted quite badly to it for a while. In that case, there can be no individual happiness forever! Damn the world! I'll become happy all alone and prove him wrong! And I wrote a poem, "A Happy Man":

> A happy man is foppish.
> A happy man has nothing to talk about.
> A happy man is odd man out.
> A happy man is all alone
>
> . . .

I wrote this, but I don't think I was happy after all.

A church in Greenwich Village, New York, cavernous, rundown, its inside's packed with men and women. Long hair bundled behind his neck, bearded, smallish Gary Snyder, with a quiet smile, reads English translations of Miyazawa Kenji. "Some Views Concerning the Proposed Site of a National Park." After reading it as if slowly chewing it as he savors it, he talks about Miyazawa Kenji from an ecological viewpoint. Snyder's book of poems called *The Back Country* includes eighteen of Kenji's poems in his own English translation. I secretly marvel at Snyder's good sense in his selection.

It's said that Reverend Tapping praised Kenji's English pronunciation. What kind of English did he speak? Like Snyder in Japanese, did he concisely say what he wanted to say, skillfully using simple vocabulary? The reading over, I approached the church door. A couple of young men were silently accepting donations, their hats held upside down. A bit like begging monks.

I entered my father's room and see a number of large sheets of paper spread all over the tatami with "First let us together turn into zillions of glittering particles in the cosmos and scatter into the directionless sky" written on them by him in ink and brush. Suddenly I had the mysterious sense of my own body transforming itself into these words and scattering like a splash of water, myself dispersing through space, the air so thin it's almost nothingness, with the speed of light, away into the distance, there was a kind of bliss in it. I had turned into zillions of particles, but I was I. I was going away, separated from the other zillion particles. I felt incomprehensible tears well up in my chest.

I have yet to see the monument, behind the town office of
Matsukawa-chō, with these words of Kenji's engraved on it.

• 5/30/1977 •

NOTES

Born in 1931, Tanikawa has remained immensely popular since publishing his
first book of poems, *Nijū-oku kōnen no kodoku* (Two billion light years of soli-
tude), in 1952. In fact, he is one of the few Japanese poets who have made a liv-
ing as a poet, without teaching at a college, for example. His father, Tetsuzō, a
philosopher and the president of Hōsei University, became famous, among the
readers and students of Kenji, for his remarks and writings, which in essence
contended that Kenji was a saint. This short essay appeared in the monthly
magazine *Eureka* special on Miyazawa Kenji (September 1977), 25–27.

1   A tatami guest room, usually spacious and airy.

2   *Ramma,* a decorative partition placed near the ceiling. It is often made of a
wood paneling with brattices.

3   A guest room boy or girl who appears to be there but isn't. In the Tōhoku di-
alect, *bokko* means "boy" or "adolescent," male or female. Although in folktales
from other regions they are mature women with long hair or boys who pull
pranks, in the main they are adolescents regarded as guardian deities of old
households: as long as they stay with you, your household thrives; if they leave,
it declines. Miyazawa wrote a story describing four different kinds of *zashiki
bokko.*

4   Kenji's story of self-sacrifice, here used as the title tale. Budori, the protagonist
with the vaguely Russian-sounding name who grew up in a famine-prone re-
gion, kills himself while artificially making a volcano erupt; he does this to let
carbon spew into the jet stream to raise the atmospheric temperature and pre-
vent the cold weather that brings crop failure.

WE ARE ALL EXCELLENT
MUSICAL INSTRUMENTS

YOSHIMASU GŌZŌ

I am entering it from a slight, door. From a slightly open door, . . . It, there, may be where the core of the fragrance of the flower has gone. (No interlinear annotations please, . . . Use ordinary writing, would you, . . . So I was told, I know, but, well, no matter how I try, my heart ends up sliding toward the delicate branches and leaves — but they are my important pleasure, the branch-leaves, . . . I'll try to make it as small in volume as I can, Ōhara-san (Mr. Ōhara Tetsuo — the person in charge of editing when this first saw print), please allow me to insert them a little, little by little. These too are music. *Notations*. Notes) A door to memory or rather what's absolutely needed to live (absolutely needed to enliven a "description," . . .) shall I call that a door, too?

Among the customs from the old days was one, I hear, that let household fixtures around you (chests and staircases, brushwood garden doors, bowls too, . . .) grow old. Wonder what it is, . . . It was surely, to keep (today's, . . .) memories polished in a new light, wasn't it? The locution "To keep memories polished in a new light, . . ." is, how shall I put it, like a string twisted and sprung into the sky, . . . I know it is an odd way of putting it but, . . . I have a fond memory of the *grainy* feel of polishing powder, . . . , then, suddenly I recall. Near the core of Kenji's ear "swishh swishh" (swishh swishh the sound of a broom = "Stories of *Zashiki Bokko*")[1] the tatami grain too is close to his eyes and nose, I suddenly think that instant, . . . (I see near my nose is the lad, . . .) such closeness that instant the now, to get close to it, I'll see what might happen if I enter my, slight door.

(I've used it as a metaphor, this "door," . . .) the door to a guest room lad or to an old house in the Northeast, . . . Drawn to the look of the house, I may be walking toward "the innermost door," . . . Of a sudden, I wrote down "keep polished in a new light, . . ." and I think I managed to get hold of the feel of some household fixtures and the polishing powder and my hands washing them as I crouch by a brook, but this "light, . . ." remains hidden. Like a "phantom house *(Tales from Tōno),*"[2] . . . I do, . . . And, "flower, . . ." (when I wrote it as a simile at the outset of this prose, I didn't notice it, . . .) called forth Hanamaki "Flower Swirl" (and Kazuno "Deer Horn" and Hanawa "Flower Wreath," Hachimandaira "Eight-flag Plateau," these place names, . . . contain mysteries, . . . *Fuminori-san,* . . .) / or perhaps was about to call it forth. As if by entering the "door" of a "phantom house," I were to expose, (breach, . . .) something.

•

I had transported with me cards and letters, several of them, the ones from musicians (Mr. Hayashi Hikaru, Takemitsu Tōru-san, Mr. Shibata Minao, . . .) If in the midst of writing this manuscript (rather than "in the midst of," it's more like, I'd say, the instant of "walking by it alone" or "standing trembling," as Kenji-san had written in the preface to *A Restaurant with Many Orders,* . . .) communicating, often interrupted, with these letters and cards, I manage to report, as if whispering to you, on the history of taking part in the creation of a CD and the process of making it, I'll be happy. Whether I can or cannot, . . . whether I can finish writing out,

separate from the voice sound of recitation, "melodies . . . unheard"
(Keats), . . . , that's my test, . . . or rather my work or task. Neverthe-
less, who can read out an "odd card" like this?

One Saturday evening an odd card came to Ichirō's house.

Mr. Kaneta Ichirō September 19
I hear you are doing fin, that good.
Because we do a complicate trial, tomorrow, pleas
come. *Don* carry a shootin tool.

Sincerely, Wildcat

("Acorns and the Wildcat," [3] *italics added)*

I italicized one spot in "the Wildcat's card," and a weird, . . . in-
describable, feeling, as if I rapped l-i-i-ghtly "the door to a dream," the
feeling of a "draft, . . ." for a "sketch" "'mental sketch'" (Kenji-san),
the feeling that I touched, . . . most likely its very edge, that tactile
sense did not fade for a while. In "How the Deer Dance Started,"[4]
around "a hand towel forgotten in solitary fashion, . . ." the deer were
circling forming a large ring, their olfactory sense, their tactile sense,
my senses may be getting closer to them, . . . and so I hastened to look
at the text and, yeah, this, too, like "a draft, . . . lies there as dropped,"
it is, . . .

his white towel next to it which lay on the grass V-shaped. . . .

This one line, stands. "lay . . . V-shaped," I saw it for an instant. . . .

A long letter came from Hayashi Hikaru-san; I look at its end and it's
dated "1997.2.8" ("date," "data," or "drought," was also an important marker for
Kenji-san as well. . . . Come to think of it, I can also "read" "weather ring" by put-
ting it in the "series," . . .), so three and a half years have passed since he

kindly sent me the letter. That letter has lain in a corner of the sofa in my room, like a silk cocoon tinged with some thin gray light, . . . The blurry fear of the spot where the letter is (what kind of simile Kenji-san might, . . . wondering, I look at "The Snow on Saddle Mountain," and there, "it's really a yeasty,/ blurry blizzard," so the border between simile and description is astonishingly soft, . . . Yes, you are right, such "natural gift, . . ." "an astonishingly soft horizon, . . ." One can't really convey it by reading it aloud, . . . "bo fū no . . . oborona fubuki," . . . One notices consecutive dull sounds, only when one is "writing" like this. Places that are "posha posha shitari kusundari," . . . well, listen to them yourself, with your own ears, like "Talking with Your Eyes,". . . .) . . . . I went to Ōsawa Hot Springs, (the old) Kikusui Pavilion, with Ōhara Tetsuo-san and Horiuchi Ken'ichirō-san, twice, and in the room (Plum — 2) at the end of the looong hall was reading "The Morning of Last Farewell" and others, not so much because we were nearing "Kenji's hometown," as because we ourselves couldn't live without approaching "my own surroundings, . . ." and that was how the pro — cess of the work on this CD production started (I practically forced them to, and they kindly agreed (gratitude, . . .). In Ōsawa Hot Springs, in Kikusui Pavilion (the old), at the dead end of its hall I opened the glass door and stuck out the "Notebook" that I'd purchased at the Kenji Museum, . . . (in the end, as a gift for my friends, I bought more than ten copies of the reproduction of the "Notebook" — because it was 500 yen a copy it was a considerable expenditure (6,000 yen for twelve copies), but the smallness of the "Notebook" so purchased, the lightness of the "memo," its softness, it was because of the "ambulatory sense" and the "bounciness" typical of Kenji, . . .) and was reading, along with the purling of the Ōsawa River, "Not yielding to rain (November 3rd)." From outside Horiuchi-san was letting a microphone dance, . . . The refreshing breeze I sensed on my cheeks at the time, the voices of birds and the purling my ears heard (. . . the microphone Horiuchi-san stuck out toward me, was like a graft or a perch . . . like a stadium for Paralympics, and that, . . .) led the scene/lump of memories of *"Not yielding to rain,"* to "another entrance," . . . (The movements of memories/active, . . . can be spelled out only in these "interlinear annotations," only as "interlinear annotations," maybe, . . . I'd guess those my age will "remember." In my case, in third or fourth grade (twenty-third or twenty-fourth year of Shōwa). I was made to do choral reading of "Not yielding to rain," was slapped, was made to stand in the corner, and was made to remain after school. It now occurs to me that it was not so much "recitation" or "chorus," as "choral reading," and I'm surprised. The young teacher, his eyes flashing with anger, in his heart, still had some traces of "choral reading," . . . Now, suddenly, I feel I understand that, . . . And "dislike of chorus" which I'm aware of somewhere in my heart was this "chorus reading," that now becomes clear to me. Come, that's, enough. I, too, should ask to be admitted to the "Devil's Tongue Troupe," perhaps, . . .)

NOTES

Born in 1939, Yoshimasu has remained at the forefront of avant-garde poetry in Japan since the publication of his first book of poems, *Shuppatsu* (Starting out), in 1964. His writings, both poetry and prose, often turn on word and sound associations and frequently employ a range of typographical variations. "We Are All Excellent Musical Instruments" is an extended essay that partly describes the process of creating, in 2000, a CD recording Yoshimasu's interactions with Miyazawa. The original essay, *Watakushi-tachi wa dare demo ga sugureta gakki nanoda,* is included in his book *Hakidashi no no no hana* (Iwanami Shoten, 2001). The translated excerpts here make up about one seventh of the original.

1 See the note on *zashiki bokko* in the previous essay.

2 *Tōno monogatari,* a collection of folklore about Tōno, a region east of Hanamaki, which Yanagita Kunio (1875–1962) published in 1910. Virtually the entire collection was based on the tales that Sasaki Kizen (1886–1933), who was from Tōno, told Yanagita, but Yanagita retold them in concise, elegant classical language as he wrote them down. He printed the book at his own expense,

in a limited edition of three hundred and fifty copies, but the slim volume became a milestone in Japanese ethnological studies. A "phantom house," *mayoiga,* is a mansion you stumble into in the depths of mountains. Although you see no one around, sometimes you see a whole banquet laid out, obviously for a large number of people. Afterward you try to find the same house, but you cannot.

3 *Donguri to Yamaneko,* the first story in *A Restaurant with Many Orders.* The card from the wildcat opens the story.

4 *Shika-odori no hajimari,* another story in *A Restaurant with Many Orders.*

MIYAZAWA KENJI

MICHAEL O'BRIEN

No lack of reasons to like and admire his poems. The wildly different vocabularies that live side by side in them — religious, technical, scientific, official — keep you on your toes, dispel habit and routine. Every page makes it clear that in them there's no such thing as the poetic, for then there would have to be the unpoetic, which would have to be avoided, and these poems exclude and avoid nothing. The opposite of hothouse work, they dwell among others, like those of William Carlos Williams, another busy man who wrote on the run. They're as devout as the poems of George Herbert and Gerard Manley Hopkins, not least in their pervasive conviction of the overwhelming *gift* of life. They're full of the most touching tenderness, as if to lose access to that would be to lose everything:

Since it's her duty,
spring comes, blue, uncomplaining.

His world was the world of "the hard-pressed farmers whose sorrows he shared and did his best to assuage," as Burton Watson once put it. Chekhov comes to mind. One poem speaks of

. . . these pieces of paper . . .
each a chain of shadow and light,
a sketch of the imagination as it is

They have a quiet exactness, most uncommon:

The electric poles cast bumpy shadows
in the fields already plowed.

which stems from endlessly patient and alert observation. They're
as intimate with creation as D. H. Lawrence's best poems. Some, such
as "Spring & Asura," have a fierce, demonic energy; others, such as
"Sapporo City," the most delicate, glancing presence:

The gray light avalanched in the distance.
Over the sand of the distorted square
I scattered sorrows like blue myths
but the birds would not touch them.

Presence is everything in these poems — an immediate world. They
astonished me when I read Hiroaki Sato's early translations of them
in the 1970s, and they still do. In the world of poetry there are the lines
you set out to memorize and the lines you are surprised to find that
you know: in the course of thirty years

In the spring, oh in the spring,
wasn't that bright love itself?

has floated up unbidden, as needed.

ASURA. In Buddhism, beings that come between beasts and human beings or their realm. The concept originally came from Indian mythology, in which the word *asura* at first meant "life-giver" (*asu* = "life" + *ra* = "give"). This was then interpreted to mean "non-or antiheavenly being" (*a* = "non" or "anti" + *sura* = "heaven"), generating the notions of asuras as demons and of battles between devas, or deities, and asuras in Hindu mythology (Iwanami edition of the *Hokkekyō* [1962], vol. 1, 378). But the positive connotation of this class of beings remains as well. As another glossary puts it, they "constitute one of the eight kinds of nonhuman beings who protect Buddhism" (Burton Watson, trans., *The Lotus Sutra* [Columbia University Press, 1993], 327). Yet another definition says: "Elemental forces, projections of the forces in man's mind" (Christmas Humphreys, *A Popular Dictionary of Buddhism* [The Citadel Press, 1963], 36).

BONNŌ (*kleśa* in Sanskrit). "Hindrances," things that prevent you from "being awakened." There are a number of categories; some say there are 108 hindrances, some say there are as many as eighty-four thousand.

BUNGO. Literary language.

BUNGOSHI. A poem in literary language.

DAIMOKU. A Nichiren-shū prayer meaning "Praise to the Sutra of the Lotus Flower of the Wonderful Dharma." See also *nembutsu*.

GŌ. A measuring unit equal to 0.38 pints.

HAGIWARA SAKUTARŌ (1886–1942). A poet whose first book, *Tsuki ni hoeru (Howling at the Moon)*, published in 1917, is regarded as a landmark — "epochal," in his own assessment — in the development of poetry in colloquial language in Japan. It spelled out so-called modern angst through a nightmarish or hallucinatory use of language.

HOKKE or HOKE. An abbreviation of *Hokke-kyō* or *Hoke-kyō*, the Lotus Sutra.

HOSAKA KANAI (1896–1937). Kenji's closest friend; he became estranged as a result of Kenji's insistent attempt to convert him to the Nichiren-shū.

ICHI. Kenji's mother (1877–1963).

KEGON-KYŌ or Avatamsaka Sutra. A text representative of the sutras in early Mahayana Buddhism.

KLEŚA. See *bonnō*.

KŌGO. Colloquial language.

KOKUCHŪKAI. See Tanaka Chigaku.

KŌTARŌ. See Takamura Kōtarō.

KUSANO SHIMPEI (1903–1988). A poet who became an ardent fan and promoter of Kenji. He started his first poetry magazine, *Dora* (Gong), in Guangdong, in 1925, and his second, *Rekitei* (Historical process), in 1935. He is famous for his frog poems, for his innovative use of onomatopoeia, and for his unique use of punctuation.

MASAJIRŌ. Kenji's father (1874–1957).

MORI SAICHI (1904–1999). A poet, writer, and editor. Mori wrote several books about Kenji. The poem partially quoted in the introduction was so realistic that some initial readers wondered whether it was a poem, as Mori intended it, or a newspaper article, though it was lineated and included futurist typographical play. Misa, one of Mori's daughters, distressed by the daily meals enumerated in the poem, once asked him if he had actually observed the family as described in the poem. He answered no, but he had grown up in terrible poverty, and his descriptions were evidently close to reality.

NEMBUTSU. "Praise to Amida Buddha." In *Ichimai kishōmon* (One-page testament), Hōnen says: "There is nothing special [about religious faith] except to assume that you will be reborn in Paradise without doubt by simply saying *Namu Amida-butsu* (Praise to Amida Buddha) and say it." *Amida* (in Sanskrit, *Amita*), comes from *Amitayus,* or *Amitabha,* meaning "eternal (immeasurable) light" or "eternal life" (Nakamura Hajime, et al., *Jōdo sambu kyō, ge* [Iwanami Shoten, 1990], 160–61).

ŌTANI KŌZUI (1876–1948). The twenty-second head of the Nishi-Honganji branch of the Jōdo Shinshū. He resigned that post in 1914 as a result of scandals but remained active in Buddhist scholarship and other cultural activities in Shanghai, Taiwan, and elsewhere.

SAKUTARŌ. See Hagiwara Sakutarō.

SEIROKU. Kenji's younger brother (1904–2001). Throughout his life he was an indefatigable promoter of Kenji.

SEKI TOYOTARŌ (1868–1955). Kenji's advisor at the Morioka Higher School for Agriculture and Forestry. An authority on volcanic ash, he brought the idea of using pulverized limestone as a fertilizer from Germany, where he studied.

SHIMAJI TAITŌ (1875–1927). A Jōdo Shinshū scholar-monk at the Gankyō-ji temple in Morioka and an authority on Kegon and

Tendai teachings. He taught at Tōyō University and at the Imperial University of Tokyo.

SHIMPEI. See Kusano Shimpei.

SHINSHŌ. It may mean what one sees in one's mind, but the term's exact origins are unknown. In his biography of Kenji, Sakai Chūichi has suggested that Kenji's hallucinatory and synesthetic tendency, on which his idea of *shinshō* may have been based, can be explained by the German psychologist E. R. Jaensch's theory of *Eidekiter,* "intuitive image."

SHŌ. A measuring unit equal to 3.8 pints.

SUZUKI TŌZŌ (1891–1961). The founder of a limestone-pulverizing company and Kenji's employer, he wrote books on how poverty in rural areas might be alleviated.

TAKACHIO CHIYŌ (1883–1976). An executive and a professor of the Kokuchūkai.

TAKAMURA KŌTARŌ (1883–1956). A sculptor's son, Kōtarō had studied art in New York and Paris from 1906 to 1909 and returned to Japan a strong advocate of Western ideals. His first book of poems, *Dōtei* (Process), published in 1914, established him as an important poet owing to his use of colloquial language in his poetry. During the 1930s he grew nationalistic and after the war was accused of supporting Japan's militaristic policy.

TANAKA CHIGAKU (1861–1939). A charismatic Nichiren-shū leader and the founder of the ultranationalistic Kokuchūkai (the Pillar of the Nation Society) who captivated Kenji. He advocated *tengyō,* "heaven's task," Japan's manifest destiny. He also coined the term *hakkō ichiu,* "all countries under one roof," which was adopted as Japan's international slogan in 1940.

TŌHOKU (Northeast). The northern part of Japan's largest island, Honshū.

ZAIBATSU. A large, family-owned industrial combine. After Japan's defeat in the Second World War, the American Occupation dissolved *zaibatsu,* albeit not too successfully.

ZENSHŪ. "Complete works." In putting together all the writings of an author, Japanese publishers are said to be like those in Russia and China: they try to include every scrap of writing left.

A great many articles and books continue to be published about Miyazawa Kenji. At least two organizations are devoted to him: the Miyazawa Kenji Museum and the Miyazawa Kenji Association Iihatov Center (the latter with a bibliography on the Internet), as well as two online sites, Miyazawa Kenji no Shi no Sekai: Mental Sketch Modified (www.ihatov.co) and Miyazawa Kenji (www.bekkoame.ne.jp/~kakurai/kenji/kenji.htm). In the following bibliography, Japanese publishers are all in Tokyo.

BY MIYAZAWA KENJI

IN JAPANESE

Few Japanese poets have enjoyed the publication of so many *zenshū*, "complete works." The first three-volume attempt, 1934–1935, was followed by a six-volume set (plus one supplementary volume), 1939–1944, by Jūjiya Shoten; a planned but not completed eleven-volume attempt, 1947–1949, by an educational union; an eleven-volume series (plus one supplementary volume), 1956–1958, by Chikuma Shobō; a twelve-volume series (plus one supplementary volume), 1967–1969; a fourteen-volume, fifteen-book *kōhon* (collated) series, 1973–1977; a sixteen-volume (plus one supplementary volume) *shinshū* (newly corrected) series, 1979–1980; a ten-volume set, the first eight in 1986 and last two in 1995; and a sixteen-volume, eighteen-book, one-supplementary series *shin-kōhon* (newly collated), beginning 1995, all published by 2004 except the supplementary volume — all by Chikuma Shobō. Small selections in paperback are available from several major houses.

IN ENGLISH

Bester, John, trans. *Kenji Miyazawa: Winds from Afar*. Tokyo and Palo Alto: Kodansha International, 1972. Sixteen of Miyazawa's stories, with graphic art by Bernard Leach.

———. *Once and Forever: The Tales of Kenji Miyazawa*. Tokyo: Kodansha International, 1994. Twenty-four of Miyazawa's stories. An expanded edition of *Winds from Afar*. This English translation has apparently been translated into German as *Die Früchte des Gingko*, with a subtitle meaning "fairy tales from Northern Japan."

Pulvers, Roger, trans. *Kenji Miyazawa: Poems*. Chikuma Shobō, 1997. Bilingual edition.

———. *Kenji Miyazawa's Night on the Milky Way Train*. Chikuma Shobō, 1996. Bilingual edition.

Sato Hiroaki, trans. *A Future of Ice: Poems and Stories of a Japanese Buddhist, Miyazawa Kenji*. San Francisco: North Point Press, 1989.

———. *Spring & Asura: Poems of Kenji Miyazawa*. Chicago: Chicago Review Press, 1973.

Sigrist, Joseph, and D. M. Stroud, trans. *Kenji Miyazawa: Milky Way Railroad*. Berkeley: Stone Bridge Press, 1996.

Snyder, Gary, ed. *The Back Country*. New York: New Directions, 1967. Includes translations of eighteen Miyazawa poems.

———. *The Gary Snyder Reader: Prose, Poetry, and Translations*. Washington, DC: Counterpoint, 1999. The five translations in this volume were first included in *The Back Country*.

Strong, Sarah M., trans., and with commentary by. *Night of the Milky Way Railway by Miyazawa Kenji: A Translation and Guide*. Armonk, NY: M. E. Sharpe, 1991.

Suzuki Ruriko, trans., with introductions by David Chandler. *Kenji Miyazawa: An Asura in Spring*. Shōhakusha, 1999. Bilingual edition.

Ueda Makoto. *Modern Japanese Writers and the Nature of Literature*. Palo Alto: Stanford University Press, 1983. One of the eight writers (all poets) discussed and analyzed is Miyazawa; this volume includes a number of poems in Ueda's translation.

Amazawa Taijirō. *Miyazawa Kenji no kanata e*. Shichōsha, 1977. Essays by a premier Miyazawa editor.

————. *Miyazawa Kenji no sekai*. NHK Shuppan Kyōkai, 1988. A series of lectures on NHK's educational TV program.

Aoe Shunjirō. *Miyazawa Kenji: shura ni ikiru*. Kōdansha, 1974. A concise, quirky biography.

Gendaishi tokuhon 12: Miyazawa Kenji. Shichōsha, 1979. A collection of essays with a selection of Kenji's poems, a bibliography, and a chronology.

Hara Shirō, ed. *Miyazawa Kenji goi jiten: Glossary Dictionary of Miyazawa Kenji*. Tokyo Shoten, 1989. More than seven hundred pages long, this glossary includes a chronology, maps, a bibliography, and an index.

Hosoi Hakaru, ed. *Iwate-ken no rekishi*. Kawade Shobō Shinsha, 1995. An illustrated history of Iwate Prefecture.

Inoue Hisashi. *Iihatōbo no geki-ressha*. Shinchōsha, 1980. A play dramatizing Miyazawa's yearnings to leave Iwate and live in Tokyo. In one passage Inoue pokes fun at *nembutsu* and *daimoku*.

————. *Miyazawa Kenji ni kiku*. Bungei Shunjū, 2002. A collection of essays and talks by Inoue and several other writers, edited by Inoue's theatrical group, Komatsu-za.

Miyagi Kazuo. *Miyazawa Kenji no shōgai: ishi to tsuchi e no yume*. Chikuma Shobō, 1980. A mineralogist's evaluation of Kenji as a geologist.

Miyazawa Kenji. The monthly *Eureka* special, 1970.

Miyazawa Kenji. The monthly *Eureka* special, 1977.

Miyazawa Kenji no sekai-ten. An exhibition catalog published to commemorate Miyazawa's hundredth birthday. Asahi Shimbunsha, 1995.

Morita, James R. *Kenji sōmei: essays on Miyazawa Kenji*. Yūseidō, 1988. A collection of essays by thirteen writers outside Japan.

Nakamura Minoru. *Miyazawa Kenji*. Shichiyōsha, 1963. One poet's assessment of another poet. Nakamura's *Miyazawa Kenji* (Chikuma Shobō, 1972) is a somewhat revised, expanded edition of the same.

Ogura Toyofumi. *"Ame nimo makezu" shinkō*. Tokyo Sōgensha, 1980. A close analysis of Kenji's pocket notebook in which he wrote "October 20th" and "November 3rd," among other things.

Ōshima Hiroyuki. *Miyazawa Kenji no shūkyō sekai*. Keisuisha, 1992. A collection of essays on Kenji's religious beliefs.

Sakai Chūichi. *Hyōden: Miyazawa Kenji*. Ōfūsha, 1968. An essential biography.

Tanikawa Tetsuzō. *Miyazawa Kenji no sekai*. Hōsei Daigaku Shuppankyoku, 1970. A collection of five talks the philosopher Tanikawa gave from 1944 to 1959. In his 1959 talk he took the poet Nakamura Minoru to task for characterizing "November 3rd" as "defeatist." Nakamura shot back in the expanded edition of his *Miyazawa Kenji*.

Terauchi Daikichi. *Kejō no Shōwa-shi*, 2 vols. Mainichi Shimbunsha, 1988. A fictionalized account of the early part of Shōwa Era (1926–1989), with a focus on how the Nichiren-shū may have influenced it. Kenji figures in it only briefly but in a full religious context.

Yoshida Tsukasa. *Miyazawa Kenji satsujin jiken*. Ōta Shuppan, 1997. A highly critical look at Kenji.

Yoshimoto Takaaki. *Higeki no kaidoku*. Chikuma Shobō, 1979. A collection of essays on five modern Japanese writers, Miyazawa among them.

ACKNOWLEDGMENTS

"A Modernist in the Mountains," by Geoffrey O'Brien, from *Bardic Deadlines: Reviewing Poetry, 1984–95* (Ann Arbor: University of Michigan Press, 1998). Reprinted by permission of the University of Michigan Press, with slight modifications by O'Brien. Originally published in the *Village Voice*.

Inoue Hisashi's description of Miyazawa as an aspiring peasant, pp. 30–31, translated by permission of the author.

"Thief," "Cloud Semaphore," "A Break," "Pine Needles," "Cow," "Some Views Concerning the Proposed Site of a National Park," "Distant Labor," and "The Politicians," by Gary Snyder, from *The Back Country*, copyright © 1968 by Gary Snyder. Reprinted by permission of New Directions Publishing Corp.

Untitled translation from Makoto Ueda's *Modern Japanese Poets and the Nature of Literature,* copyright © 1983 by the Board of Trustees of the Leland Stanford Jr. University. Reprinted by permission.

Tanikawa Shuntarō's essay translated by permission of the poet.

Excerpts from Yoshimasu Gōzō's essay translated by permission of the poet.

Michael O'Brien's article printed by permission of the poet. Some of the verses he quotes are from my translation of *Spring & Asura* (Chicago: Chicago Review Press, 1973).

I wish to thank Kakizaki Seiji for preparing six of the photos used as illustrations, Kakizaki Shōko for helping to collect books, and Tachibana Ken'ichirō for helping to collect information on various matters.

I first translated Miyazawa Kenji's poems with Michael O'Brien in the early 1970s, and the translations, incorporating Burton Watson's many suggestions, were published in *Spring & Asura*. When Jack Shoemaker agreed to publish an expanded edition, with stories added, I revised the earlier translations; as I translated more poems, my sense of the importance of being faithful to the original had grown. *A Future of Ice* was the result. But with many of the translations I have no doubt that some readers will prefer the earlier versions. Here I have limited extensive revisions to a few in *A Future of Ice*.

I thank Gene Reeves, Nancy Rossiter, and Robert Fagan for reading the new manuscript closely and for giving me a number of helpful comments. Mr. Reeves also allowed me to cite from his unpublished translation of the Lotus Sutra. And I thank Jerome Rothenberg, Pierre Joris, and Laura Cerruti for including Miyazawa Kenji in the Poets for the Millennium series.

TEXT:	10.75/15 GRANJON
DISPLAY:	AKZIDENZ GROTESK
COMPOSITOR:	BOOKMATTERS, BERKELEY
PRINTER AND BINDER:	THOMSON-SHORE, INC.